The thread

Infanta of Spain Eulalia

Alpha Editions

This edition published in 2023

ISBN : 9789357940795

Design and Setting By
Alpha Editions
www.alphaedis.com
Email - info@alphaedis.com

Contents

PREFACE

SOME preface, however short, is needed to this book, the mirror of some of my ideas, and, first of all, I wish to put my readers on their guard against a false interpretation of the motives by which I have been actuated.

In publishing these opinions of mine, it has not been my wish to accomplish a literary work. I have not aimed at any display of learning, and I make no pretence of forcing on anyone my different points of view.

As a spectator in close enough contact with present social problems to understand all the points under discussion, yet at the same time sufficiently removed from them to analyse them coolly and judge them without prejudice, I bring forward my evidence unshackled by conventions. It has seemed to me that such fair, exact evidence might interest those who seek to glean, amongst all classes of society, the thousand dissimilar and contradictory elements whence proceed the lessons needed both for the present and the future.

Those who care to glance through the short chapters of this book will soon see that they have been written with the sincere conviction with which I always express my ideas and opinions, or perform any work independently undertaken.

I only ask my readers to excuse any faults of style, which I have tried to make up for by straightforwardness of tone.

EULALIA
Infanta of Spain

GENERAL CAUSES OF HAPPINESS

THE most imperative motive of all human actions is the desire to be happy. But it is difficult to attain happiness if the search for it is made the constant aim of one's life, although the primordial craving for it is an instinct in our nature.

The art of living is one in which we are but ill instructed by philosophers, scientists and metaphysicians; the first, because they leave the meaning of life as it is to show us some end in view; the second, because they are but rationalist theorists; and the last, because they claim to be able to lift the veil from the Beyond. The truth is that life is worth living, and that in order to live happily one must know how to draw from life a relative amount of happiness.

Simply by realising the charm of the pleasures—small though they be—which every instant of the day offers us, one may create for oneself a source of happiness, for this realisation gives what is usually called the *joie de vivre* (the joy of living), the principle in all happy nature.

Unfortunately, in the majority of cases, man does not see clearly the road leading to happiness because he is seeking it in the immediate and complete satisfaction of his desires, in material or intellectual delights whose worth he exaggerates; in superfluity, in possession, in all that he takes for happiness, but which is in reality mere enjoyment allied to fears, dangers, and regrets.

It is necessary, first of all, to simplify the causes of happiness. To illustrate my doctrine, I ask everyone to imagine the idyll in its true form, that is to say, as being the perfect presentment of the sentiment of love. Simplicity, whether in personal tastes, in the affections, or in daily actions, is the great secret of happiness.

With our nature, however justifiable it may be to acquaint ourselves with partial and transitory satisfactions, we cannot build up happiness on so fragile a foundation. Fortune is unstable; notoriety, whatever its cause, fades with time; glory is a vain word; health declines, and all is ruin and sorrow everywhere, save where complete satisfaction has been built up by continually aspiring towards the True, the Beautiful, and the Good.

Again, that aspiring must be the result of cultivating, in all simplicity, our mental "*I*." Happiness lies in the depths of ourselves; it is by the right development of our personality that we may bring it into manifestation, make of it the enfolding comfort of our days.

Is it not true, that in love, if you live in the spirit, you possess more happiness than if you live in the senses? It is the same with material existence; simplified, reduced to the normal exercise of our faculties, it brings us a greater share of happiness than does excess. All the vices of our nature furnish but a momentary satisfaction, and that not unmixed with bitterness.

But how shall we attain to the development of our mental personality? First of all by the training of our Self, then by the selection of affinities. In this way each one, conscious of his own true desires, may bring around him those whose tastes and feelings are in harmony with his own. So may he avoid the painful and regrettable shocks and collisions which lead fatally to strife, from which combative and provocative natures cannot emerge without wounds, weariness, or disgust.

If you are obliged to live in a country different from your own, or amid surroundings where the mental atmosphere does not harmonise with yours, face the situation coolly; learn to be by turns the wise teacher and the willing disciple: in this way you will become understood, appreciated, and you will preserve intact your inner happiness.

You must learn to pass through moral and intellectual atmospheres as you pass through those of the physical world. Just as you put on the costume suitable to the season, so must your spirit assume the costume adapted to its surroundings. Many people fear life, they are in despair over the least ill-success; they tack about, dreading to enter the haven, and their mistakes vex and disconcert them. Remember that there is no circumstance which should cast you down or prevent your enjoying life, because, I repeat, happiness is inward content, a supporting spirit which one may attain in spite of the worst vicissitudes or unavoidable catastrophes. Since inward happiness proceeds from a habit of character produced by the training of oneself, the cultivation of simplicity, and adapting oneself to the uncongenial, it is necessary to submit to these things if one would steer his barque skilfully and taste all that constitutes the supreme enjoyment of life.

He who has followed these precepts will be able, when his days begin to decline, to look back calmly on the past. As he has drawn from every circumstance in his life the greatest possible good, as he will possess the certainty of having injured no one, he will see with infinite tranquillity the gates of Death opening before him; more especially if he has also cultivated a love of Nature, for the pleasure it gives by its restfulness and its eternal loveliness.

THE EDUCATION OF THE WILL

THE will is the faculty of freely determining to do certain actions. But in order that the will may always be the result of ideas noble in aim, it is necessary to give it some training, through the investigation of conflicting causes and motives.

As Ribot says: "The *I will* declares a situation, but does not constitute one." To constitute a situation requires the formation of character, which is nothing more than will power. And this may be obtained by a progressive training, the secret cultivation of one's personality.

The human being should impress upon all his actions a unity of aim, and show forth his character in what he does.

The education of the will, then, is indispensable in life, if only for the avoidance of useless effort and to give us clearness of moral sight. This training brings us to the mastery of ourselves, to steady persistence in action, and uniformity of conduct. Thus considered, the will assumes paramount importance in the life of the individual, and forms one of the most powerful forces in the world—free and willing action under the control of sound judgment.

If you educate your will, *desiring that which is good, beautiful and just*, you will never undertake mental work at a time when inauspicious circumstances make it liable to failure; nothing which you undertake will remain unachieved; you will follow no aim whose fulfilment does not seem to you certain.

The immortal Guyau says: "He whose action is not in accordance with his thought, thinks incompletely." Now, in order to think completely, an idea must be solidly based upon knowledge. And knowledge is the result of the education of the will.

Let us make no mistake, such training gives us force which is invaluable. A man, having considered the action he is about to perform, perceived what will be its results, grasped its utility, and shaped it to the end in view, may safely obey his will, provided his moral sense is satisfied. He thus assumes, in full understanding, the responsibility of his actions.

The effect of this idea of responsibility is that the individual will becomes answerable to itself only. From the moment the education of the will is completed, personal determination is almost instantaneous. The result is the avoidance of loss of time—we no longer exhaust ourselves in hesitation, questionings, indecision. Besides, as we are able to bring into play, through mental use, the forces which are ours, the sense of freedom grows stronger, and with it the sense of possessing the power to attain the end in view.

The education of the will is of such utility that, without it, the intellect is powerless to influence action. That is the reason why, in these days, so many intellectual people are the victims of hesitation and doubt, incapable of reasoned and logical action.

A trained will brings great stability into a man's life, first because it enables him to do everything at the right time, then because it prevents conflicting feelings, by strengthening the reasoning powers; and, through systematised thought, saves him from those emotional storms which are as injurious to health as to free play of the will.

Let us no longer forget that all truly profitable actions and strong characters are the work of the will.

Timidity, to specify amongst qualities detrimental to the intellect, only comes from a lack of will-training, being a form of over-emotionalism without control. He who is ignorant of the laws which govern feeling, will be unable to act according to the dictates of reason.

I must make it clear that, in speaking of the education of the will, I do not mean moral restraint. The individual should feel himself at liberty, bound only by an ideal of goodness which repudiates all thought of authority; neither claiming nor suffering it.

This ideal, inseparable from our conception of what is useful both to ourselves and others, always takes form through the education of our will; giving consistency to the expression of feeling, and justifying us in our actions.

To envelop oneself in an idea, so that nothing has power to distract—to withdraw, concentrate upon it, burn for its realisation, obey its laws—such are the principal features of will-training, by means of which our actions and feelings, far from losing in strength, acquire greater force.

Violence and precipitation are foes to all wisely planned action. What one loses in intensity by calm reflection, one gains in quality as the result of this law.

If you train your will wisely, you will double the worth of existence; you will leave undone what is useless, you will realise to the full the purpose of your soul.

And, as all your actions will be performed with the approval of your own spirit, you will know the joy of well-doing.

HONESTY

HONESTY, the quality corresponding to honour, may be said to be relative, according to the customs of different countries. For mankind generally, honesty consists in not exceeding the limits of licensed dishonesty. Thus in commerce, which is, at bottom, a cheating game, integrity is not, as Dr. Dubois says, the same everywhere. "There are communities, little cultivated in other respects, where it is observed scrupulously; there are others in which, in spite of scientific, artistic and literary development, this moral perception seems to be atrophied. A people whose business honesty is proverbial may have a very elastic conscience in regard to morality between the sexes."

In the professions, or in social positions which place the individual above the mass of people, a man's honesty consists in adapting his conscience to the circumstances of the moment.

In questions of commercial or industrial enterprise, intellectual ventures, public or private morals, general or particular interests, masculine honesty is an adjustable matter which springs from the desire for free action, without infringing upon the law.

Woman's honesty is quite a different matter. It consists simply in safeguarding the "honour of the home," in keeping away all "intruders" upon the sacred ground of marriage, and in averting any fracas tending to diminish the authority of the man, the husband, the owner, and free the feminine soul from its ancestral slavery.

This is why men and women cannot be in perfect accord, so long as honesty, taken in the widest sense, is not the same for both. Based upon respect for what is fair, just and good, honesty has essentially no sex. Whether strict or comparative, it does not imply a different moral law for individuals of different natures.

This primordial question has always been treated too lightly, though it has been the source of continual misunderstanding, especially in matrimonial questions.

How many examples one could give of want of scruple violating the idea of honesty and responsibility!

How many sins, grave in themselves, are committed by men in power, knowing themselves safe from the arm of the law; how many actions, unpunishable, yet which are an outrage upon the liberty of others, a breach of respect for human nature, and an injury to society!

How many men sacrifice, for the sake of ambition, their country's vital interests, and incur no censure save that of powerless public opinion!

The orator who, in a moment of national excitement, throws his visionary dreams and interested lies broadcast into the press; the leader who, in full consciousness of his abominable work, deceives the people; the perjured politician who denies his convictions to attain promotion, should all have their honour called in question. To such as these, as to others, woman owes respect and obedience, without the option of comparing her own honour, based on imperative duty, with that of these empty talkers and tub-orators.

It is true that, on the other hand, a woman may, without censure, give out that her dearest friend's husband is making love to her—that she may thus, by a word, destroy a home's peace—without any pangs of conscience, and without the man attacked being able to call her to account.

In the relations between men and women some solution should be found by which both may be placed on equal ground as regards morality and responsibility. In this way loss of esteem between them would be avoided, and the value of each enhanced.

But, to obtain such a result, tolerance and the principle of harmony must first be taught; men must become less selfish, and women learn that their life is not only a work of love but a work of reason. Social rights must be equalised in the light of conscience and moral responsibility. In fact, thorough sincerity must bring about loyalty both in business and private affairs, creating a moral atmosphere in which forgery, fraud, plagiarism, the lie that corrupts the soul of a people, all the monstrous growths of our modern society, can no longer exist. Then honesty, from being comparative, will become supreme, incumbent equally upon man and woman, bound no longer only by social, but by moral ties.

FRIENDSHIP

FRIENDSHIP, taken in its strict sense, that is to say as affection exempt from the attraction of the senses, plays an immense part in the lives of men and women.

Friendship, as between men, is based on moral equality. The tie uniting two minds and two hearts creates the same rights and the same duties for each of the friends, no matter how different their degree of fortune and rank in the world. Where friendship is, there is reciprocity. This is what made La Boétie, Montaigne's great friend, say: "Friendship is a sacred name, it is a holy thing.... There can be no friendship where there is cruelty, disloyalty, or injustice.... The wicked are not friends, but accomplices."

I must quote here an admirable passage from Emerson, whose judgment is sound concerning what is high, great and forceful in the dual character of Friendship: "The sufficient reply to the sceptic, who doubts the power of the furniture of man, is in that possibility of joyful intercourse with persons, which makes the faith and practice of all reasonable men. I know of nothing life has to offer so satisfying as the profound good understanding which can subsist, after much exchange of good offices, between two virtuous men, each of whom is sure of himself, sure of his friend. It is a happiness which postpones all other gratifications, and makes politics, and commerce, and churches, cheap. For, when men shall meet as they ought, each a benefactor, a shower of stars, clothed with thoughts, with deeds, with accomplishments, it should be a festival of Nature which all things announce. Of such friendship, love in the sexes is the first symbol, as all other things are symbols of love. These relations to the best men—which, at one time, we reckoned the romances of youth—become, in the progress of character, the most solid enjoyment."

Friendship between women is somewhat different from that between men, just because it excludes the feeling of equality. It is very rare, in spite of the best education, that a woman will forget her rank and fortune with a friend who becomes her protégée. It is no less rare when a woman in a humble position does not resent any outward inequality. The result is that friendship between women is not a continual delightful exchange of feeling and opinion, but rests more on interest.

One of the most beautiful forms of friendship, as some think, is that between man and woman. Between persons of the highest education and refined tastes, such friendship not only plays a great part in life, but becomes a necessity, for it increases the intellectual power of both parties. It is very like disinterested love, and is governed by secret influences which give it its value. Certain people have the gift of drawing out our confidences; there are others the very sight of whom makes our heart rejoice. Our spiritual force, our eloquence, often come into play simply through the presence of such a beloved friend.

There is a peculiar feeling of confidence between the sexes; friendship between a man and a woman has something in it graver, deeper than any other. Even in family relationships, what I call "home friendship" depends entirely on this kind of mutual dependence. Cases are rare of sons turning against their mother, or of sisters who fail their brothers.

Friendship is said to be blind; I believe, on the contrary, that it is clear-sighted as to the duties entailed upon it, and needs no vow to make it binding.

If, for a man, a friend of his own sex is a second self, for a woman a man-friend is at once a confidant, a counsellor and a protector. He represents authority with reverence, incalculable devotion; he becomes the symbol of that Good which signifies refuge from suffering, forgiveness when one has erred.

For a man, a woman friend is everything; yet his feeling for her is the purest in the world, the affection which asks nothing in return.

Yet too great intimacy may kill friendship, which—to quote Emerson again—follows the laws of divine necessity; unless the things of daily life have become of common interest between the friends. But even then the friendship should be in some sort kept in a shrine apart lest it fall into the commonplace.

Yes, truly, the human heart desires a friend. It seeks him everywhere, even from childhood, and when it has found him, it is proud of him as of a victory through which it has won happiness, strength, the incentive to become better. We carry our friend's eyes in our own; in his absence, they mirror his care for us. His coming strikes a note of triumph in our brain, his presence lightens every moment and makes our happiness. Montaigne did violence to a beautiful gift of the spirit in denying the existence of friendship between men and women; and Nietzsche declares too lightly, and without taking into account the moral worth of the individual, that for the maintenance of friendship between a man and woman a little physical aversion is necessary.

Certainly, Don Juan and Ninon de Lenclos could not have been friends; but it is equally certain that a beautiful woman may win the purest friendship of a charming man, for friendship between man and woman springs from a train of circumstances which lead them into soul fellowship, the sharing of similar tastes, and an affection entirely of the spirit. The constant interchange of high thought, the brotherly and sisterly tone of the relationship, safeguard the friends against becoming lovers.

The nature of each contributes greatly, in these heart unions, to the friendship's being compatible with prudence and consideration for the feelings of others. It is obvious that a friendship begun between two people of unbalanced mind is almost always fatal, but two dissimilar natures, if morally equal, steady one another by a friendship which becomes for them a safety-valve.

For instance, a man with a calm temperament, but not a cold heart, will be the best of friends for an impulsive woman, and render her the greatest services that life can give.

Let us look at this loving friendship, so much discussed, so often described and cried down.

I said that friendship between man and woman was a form of disinterested love; it is a love based on mental sympathy, on respect for moral qualities, on admiration for certain actions or certain thoughts expressive of a character. In this kind of friendship, affection, which springs from the heart, governs love, which springs from the senses.

This form of friendship is not to be despised, dangerous though it may seem in the eyes of severe moralists or of hypocrites. Take such a case. If either of the friends needs advice on some matter he or she has deeply at heart, such advice will not be well considered, unbiased, and to the point, unless free from all jealousy—coming from the heart and not from the nerves.

Then, and then only, can this friendship be a precious resource, a deep, protective affection claiming not possession as its reward.

DIVORCE

MARRIAGE, considered by society as a necessary mode of union, is a contract governed by law.

In the eyes of Roman Catholics, marriage being a sacrament, which renders it indissoluble, divorce does not exist. According to this principle we must accept as a sacrament an earthly tie which touches more nearly on material than on spiritual questions. But it seems strange that the Church of Rome should teach men, by the voice of her servants, that human perfection consists in the acceptance of *all the sacraments*, and then forbid marriage—which would be, from a practical point of view, the most useful to them—to her representatives. In so doing, the Church creates an illogical exception to her imperious rule.

"From the psychological point of view," says Dr. Toulouse, "marriage is the union, first through passion, then through sympathy, of two beings; from the social point of view, it represents a mutual effort towards reproduction.

"The union of feeling between two beings has not been too highly exalted by the poets. It manifests in the highest degree that selection which purifies the instinct of sex.

"This selection is in itself a proof of the free will which works—with restraining effect—on the tyranny of passion. Again, the woman, in giving herself to one only, demonstrates in the most striking manner that she belongs to, and can dispose of, herself.

"Sex freedom, then, which is a condition of evolution, is manifested most clearly in a marriage entered upon willingly by both parties. But the corollary to this is, that divorce should also be possible simply at the wish of both."

Let us study divorce from the point of view of its utility. Divorce offers an advantage in preventing marriage from being regarded as an endless chain, a crushing yoke, or a prison deliberately chosen as a livelihood. It means, in fact, that people need not be tightly bound together who cannot bear so to live; it would put an end to what is sometimes extreme mental suffering, abolish dangers which sometimes lead to murder; in a word, it means escape from "the sentimental and emotional results of the indissolubility of marriage."

The termination of miserable "marriages of convenience" would ensure for many a new life, the production of healthier children under normal conditions; from the social point of view, it would increase the value of the man and the woman.

How many live together for long years who are strangers to each other in body and soul! How many slaves of marriage there are, whose union is unnatural, childless, and made hideous by mutual hatred!

Why should one see, in the name of a religious principle, these infernos—whose tortures are as varied as they are crushing—perpetuated? Why should not reason, individual rights, be allowed to correct ill-chance, false calculations, and disappointed hopes?

Why should a woman, who no longer finds in her husband the moral support she needs, submit to the horrors of a long agony without defence, of perpetual strife in which she is miserably vanquished; on the other hand, why should the man who does not find in his wife the companion—or even the slave—he desired, see the way to happiness closed to him for ever?

Marriage is based on a contract. Every contract can be rectified, modified, or broken. In a compact, there must be mutual agreement; from the moment when the agreement ceases to be respected by either of the parties, it is naturally dissolved.

Before the establishment of divorce the husband and wife who lived on bad terms had to endure suffering worse than death, for nothing, I repeat, is to be compared with the torment of being tied, body and soul, in hatred, contempt, or even merely in indifference.

In former days, the independent-minded, those who feared not public opinion, or thought little of social conventions, went each their way, to live in a different dwelling—as happens still in certain countries (in Spain, for instance, where divorce does not exist; where legal separation is not even recognised); but though they might live apart, the marriage contract held none the less, and the question of fortune remained a grave problem for solution. It is the same to-day when, through worldly expediency, or weakness, an ill-assorted couple share a miserable life or seek solace in separation. The woman, married under the Napoleonic Code, cannot dispose of her dowry, and the man, on his side, cannot sell without his wife's signature. The *société d'acquêts* (common property of married people) is a constant menace in a situation of this kind; one comes to think that it is of no use for a couple to economise for the sake of their heirs, for, when one of the two parties dies, the common property goes to the other. Another case, also serious, may occur. If either husband or wife incurs debts, these, under the law, become common to both, and it comes about that the one who has not run into debt finds him or herself compelled to meet the liabilities of the other!

What manifold complications, what openings for dissension, what accumulated vexations! Widowhood, widowerhood, seems the only deliverance from a desperate situation.

But there is something worse still. In a household completely at variance, weary with strife, the children have to look on at scenes which wound their belief in the love between husband and wife. In such a case they suffer through the absence of divorce, both from the moral standpoint and because they are deprived of property which should fall to them, since through the *société d'acquêts*—that stern claimant—the children's capital cannot be increased.

If we pass from this array of facts to another, which concerns this unnatural life of two people, the evil is no less great.

From the time when life together has become impossible, the husband more or less openly substitutes illicit union for marriage, and most frequently takes to live with him the woman he has chosen as his new companion. Because the marriage contract remains unbroken, this is an insult to the wife, for his house is still her home by law.

Although in a case of separation, the wife almost always acts with greater circumspection and caution, she will find it difficult to prevent the echo of any attention she may accept from reaching the ears of her husband, or his knowledge that she gives willingly to another what she has yielded with such aversion to himself.

Divorce prevents this gratuitous insult to marriage. The advantages it offers exceed by far the disadvantages cited by the defenders of an institution which to-day has grown weak because it has remained unchanged in the midst of social evolution.

The enemies of divorce assert that it is the destroyer of the family. That is not so, for there are no more families to destroy. Frankly, honestly, where is the family of old, since the law of the majority has freed the child, since compulsory education has lessened the moral authority of parents, without perceptibly improving the mass of the people; since in the vast field of higher education boys and girls, through school life, become strangers to the authors of their being and are mainly indebted to the State for their training?

If hypocrisy were not at the bottom of the whole matter, it would be quickly seen that nothing remains of the family as a sacred institution.

Authority on the one side, submission on the other, are the exception; the sacrifices, too, which parents made in the past, to the point of forgetting their own well-being, have to-day no longer any reason for existing.

Yes, divorce is useful, necessary, moral. But it may, it should, become more so, and undergo modification. Divorce by mutual consent must become the remedy for evils which dishonour the human soul; victims of unhappy marriages should be able to dissolve their union without the most intimate details of two lives—poisoned by misunderstanding, incompatibility of temper, excess, cruelty, and insult—being made a prey to public curiosity, the malice of barristers, and the opinions of judges. Those liberated from their matrimonial prison, and ripened by experience, must be allowed to marry the beloved one who has loved, consoled, and helped them through the battle of their days.

Nine times out of ten, these new marriages would be happy, because the husband and wife would have had time to appreciate each other's qualities, because they would have obeyed the law of love, escaped convention and not been guided, generally speaking, by interest, that chief and pernicious element in conflict between the sexes.

Divorce, as at present established, does not afford enough solutions for the melancholy problems resulting from marriage. It is inadmissible, inhuman, even immoral, that one who has suffered patiently twenty years "for the children's sake" should be condemned, because he or she has left the torture-chamber, to pass the remainder of life without the right to create a new home and consecrate by marriage the affection and devotion which have healed the old wounds, given back joy in living, and created for him or her obligations at once moral and social.

The day when divorce shall become a law of justice, and no longer—as it sometimes is now—a tacit agreement covering wrongdoing; the day when divorce shall exist by the will of him or her who gives valid reasons for it, and also by mutual consent; the day, finally, when lover and beloved, under normal conditions, may marry, then true and rightful solutions will have been brought to impossible situations, and a noble work done for the individual and society at large.

THE FAMILY

THE conditions of the modern family, in the northern countries particularly, have in reality become almost artificial; and it seems probable that, in the near future, the family will be completely disintegrated.

In France, especially amongst the *bourgeoisie*, the family appears to me likely to remain for a long time what it has been heretofore, because it constitutes an association the members of which, closely grouped, protect their common interests, whether commercial or industrial.

This family, representing a society in the possession of property, will exist as long as its members, in virtue of their fellowship, preserve intact their old social conditions, each of them continuing to have an interest in the success of their common enterprise.

In Spain, where the Moorish government has left so many traces of its primitive organisation, the family still continues in a state of slavery, a state wherein the woman glories.

But the question here is not of these two particular cases, where the maintaining of the family group serves the interests of the man, the head, the master; for the family differs according to different centres, countries, customs, and castes.

To come to more general statements, we must first go back to the fountain-head, and consider the family in its evolution through the course of civilisation.

The family, as it first appears in the history of humanity, was a patriarchal association formed of the father, mother and children. There was no binding marriage, but repeated unions. The conditions were such that the women were for all men indiscriminately, and the children knew no father in particular. This state of things in many cases continued so long that the Christian Church was obliged, at its birth, to wink at this communism. Herodotus tells us that the children of the Lycians bore the name of their mother; Varro assures us that it was the same in Athens, and that the woman, being the producer of wealth, was the only one to inherit.

When polygamy began, the woman was reduced to a state of seclusion and often of slavery. Her part consisted principally in bringing children into the world, and her care of them was more through instinct than love.

As for the man, he sought nothing, as regarded the woman, but his own gratification, and concerned himself not at all about fatherhood.

Later on, through the growth of civilisation, monogamy decided the limits of the family and formed class groups; but gradually, these groups becoming mixed and losing their old characteristic of brotherhood, the conditions of the family became much modified.

The causes of this slow process of breaking up accumulated, according to the particular centre and to social degrees. In one place primogenitureship began to take to itself privileges; in another the paternal power lessened the mother's authority over her daughters; everywhere there was a tendency towards emancipation, and, finally, in our own day, at the two poles of society, family conditions have become almost artificial.

The home peace is troubled, and even where there is no rupture between the husband and wife, there is mental friction between parents and children, between brothers and sisters, through the clash of opinion, mutual intolerance, and the collision of personal interests; it is rarely that harmony prevails in the household.

It must be said that the reasons for marriage are not the same as they were in the old days, when the bond was indissoluble, based on the instinct of ownership, on the government of a community. Besides, the marriage for love, the only one worthy of respect, has destroyed the original idea of the association, and, unable to guarantee its own continuance, calls for an adjustment of responsibilities by means of the law, so that the man shall no longer be the brutal master, and the woman—though she be more moral, more virtuous, and more temperate than he—humiliated and degraded. It has been said that it is enough for a woman to be beautiful and to be a mother. That is altogether absurd nonsense. The woman has a right to the complete development of her faculties, a right to bring into play all the resources of her being. Noble women have proved that, quite apart from maternity, they are fit to walk in the immortal footsteps of heroes, artists and thinkers, and every day we see women

THE INFANTA EULALIA
Photograph by Baumann, Munich.

becoming, in talent, energy, and patient determination, rivals of scientists, poets, and all who devote themselves to enterprise in the world of mind.

But, it may be said, such claims are contrary to the idea of the family. Not at all. The family, essentially modified, each member subject to the determinism of thought and ensuring the observance of mutual rights and duties, will only become a more beautiful institution than before, its children born of sincere love and no longer the product of undesirable or questionable unions based upon the interests of the strongest.

THE COMPLETE INDEPENDENCE OF WOMAN

TO this question squarely put: "Why does a man arrogate to himself the right to live as he chooses, and why should a woman submit to a prohibitive moral code?"—men answer that in marriage the virtue of the wife and the legitimacy of her children are absolutely and supremely essential.

This touches one point merely, and only applies to married women. In all that concerns "free" women, by what right are they condemned to abstain from making full use of their independence, as most men do? "Woman's life, like man's," says Miramont, "is a harmonious evolution, by which every phase is developed, and which thus brings into play a succession of forms and aspects of existence. Daughter, mother and grandmother; dreamer, fighter, thinker—woman, like man, passes through many transformations in the course of life, and is always progressive."

By the same fact of social evolution, thanks to her participation in the battle of life, and also to a rational education, it has long been proved that woman is not an inferior creature, of no use save for the propagation of the species.

We are far removed, happily, from the theories of Schopenhauer, who declared that woman was afflicted with intellectual shortness of sight, that she was childish, futile and narrow, inferior to man in everything concerning rectitude and scrupulous honesty; that she was lacking in sense and reflection, incapable of taking any unbiased view, etc. etc.

If woman's characteristic feature be that nature has destined her for motherhood, it is none the less true that, just as she has a fine skin and quick sensibilities, her intellect is prompt to seize details, and that she possesses a brain as well furnished as that of man.

Her apparent inferiority comes from the fact that woman is oppressed by the law and ill-treated by the moralist, whence result her native timidity and diffidence. The truth is that man, desiring to keep the supremacy attributed to him, does not care to see in woman the qualities of courage and independence. He will not admit the immanent struggle between two beings inspired by the same needs and the same desires. Men would like women to remain tied down to household cares, while thinking women who have ceased to resign themselves to this wish their sex to profit by all the rights of men.

The partisans of absolute feminism desire that there should be no difference between men and women, in the name of biological equality which incites them to claim social equality.

Without going so far as this, it is certain that women should now enjoy more independence and be authorised, without losing caste in the eyes of moralists, to prove the strength of their personal faculties.

Unfortunately, as a modern thinker has observed: "Kept apart from magnificent realities ... maintained continually in a state of moral independence worse than physical slavery, only quitting the maternal yoke to fall under that of a husband, trained entirely with a view to marriage, which is to transform at a stroke the child into the wife, the wife into the mother, educated according to the prejudices of their set at the sacrifice of expansion of their own personality, women do not develop normally, except by finding a kindred soul, according to the ideal formed in their dim consciousness. And as social conventions do not permit them to seek this ideal, which is falsified and made vague, too, by novel-reading, enlightenment usually comes to them too late to destroy the effect of a narrow existence accepted through timidity, ignorance, or chagrin, and moulded by the dictates of society; so they live, for the most part, either like children broken in to their destiny, or like rebels in search of visionary compensations: in any case misunderstood."

I have nothing better to add. For centuries, man has denied to woman her finest qualities, which are *fearlessness* and *presence of mind*, and the majority of women have come to be convinced themselves that these qualities are unwomanly and to be reckoned faults.

Now, if tenderness be woman's most beautiful attribute, it should be recognised that true tenderness is especially found amongst those women who are courageous, strong and endowed with shrewd sense. The acceptance of servitude does not admit of real tenderness, such as influences, for instance, the conception and carrying out of works of art, as incites to noble action, and produces wonderful results in every degree of the social scale.

For years, in many countries, the attention of thinkers has been fixed upon the liberation of woman. Many mistakes have been made. Against one John Stuart Mill a crowd of philosophers like Nietzsche have arisen, but the idea is gaining ground in scientific centres, and, with the help of rational Socialism, the work of woman's emancipation is being steadily pursued.

Reverting to old times, we find that in many primitive races, the males were chosen by the females for their valour, physical strength, or natural beauty. This selection having led to the progressive development of the male in the majority of races, resulted in an ideal female type also.

But when the woman became the "property" of the man, the slave destined to work for the male, the development of the race stopped short; the salutary effect of the woman's free choice having ceased.

In a new state of society, when woman, duly trained for her part, shall recover her complete freedom, we shall see the triumph of affinities, and the power of a feminine ideal will ensure for the future a new and vigorous race.

THE WAR AGAINST FEMINISM

IT is incomprehensible that so many intellectual, sensible men, claiming to be logical, should be hostile to modern feminism. I say "modern" to mark the actual state of conflict, for *eternal feminism* is contemporaneous with the *eternal feminine*, as Lucien Muhlfeld says. Following Schopenhauer and Strindberg, who strove to demonstrate the inferiority of woman, our detractors, in making war upon feminism, show themselves to be very inconsistent. As woman, is, in their eyes, an inferior being, they are either fighting what they have no reason to fear, which shows lack of courage on their part; or, by admitting that under present conditions woman plays an important part in everyday life, they recognise in her a certain value, which shows a lack of sincerity.

On the day woman first recognised the fact that she could earn her living by taking up the employments hitherto reserved for men, she made good her claim to a share of instruction and training by means of which to put an end to her mental inequality.

Unable to escape from the subordinate position in the family thrust upon her by the Civil Code, she determined to free her mind first, and gain recognition of her rights in the domain of intellect. This seemed inadmissible, even in respect of the principles of science.

Now, in times gone by, women worked as much as, and often more than, men, thus gaining recognition of their physical strength. When man was still a barbarian, hunting and fighting for mere subsistence, woman hunted and fought with him; just as his comrade, she carried the slain beast over her shoulder. Later, she spun flax to clothe her family; she was obliged, in her enslaved condition, to turn to common uses her intellect and devotion, and when, later still, the family was placed on a legal footing, she was obliged to give all her faculties to manual labour.

Long centuries passed. Man had no longer to fight for his daily bread. One invention after another had gradually modified the conditions of his life; he had become educated, had attained to different trades and professions, developed his power and authority, while woman remained the same dependent creature, tied to her duties as wife and mother. A time came when woman, too, learnt trades which she made her own. Man took them from her, possessed himself of her needle, of clothes-making, hairdressing, cookery. This is why, in the eighteenth century, women attempted an inroad into letters and the arts. This is why, helped by the Revolution, they sought to claim common rights. To-day, trained at school and college, women know that they can utilise their faculties more nobly than hitherto. They no longer live in an epoch when, men having absorbed everything, they have to resign themselves to being married, whilst hardly more than children, for a livelihood.

Consider how sad was the lot of the woman when, devoid of the means to free herself honestly from slavery, she was compelled to sell herself, by legal marriage or otherwise.

Whatever certain philosophers and anti-feminists may say, the reason why the personality of the woman weakened in the course of ages, was that her physical force had been exhausted, which entailed mental inferiority.

But through the progress of science, innovations of all kinds, economic and social evolution, daily events; throughout the complexities of a new life, woman began to make her influence felt, became conscious of her powers, strengthened by study, system and experience.

Strindberg, the misogynist, when he declared that "woman is incapable of acquiring complete knowledge in any branch of study whatsoever," said a foolish thing. In proof of the contrary, in the university, in the art schools, in law, women are said to be, if not superior to men, at least their equal.

It must be remembered that it is less than a century since woman, even in the most advanced countries, was first allowed to receive the same training as man. Taking into consideration how far behind her rival in intellect she then was, the results she has obtained give a flat contradiction to those who opposed her equality, which, originally a law of nature, has, under modern social conditions, become a law of existence.

If it be true that it takes several generations to perfect a race from a physical point of view, it is equally true that several generations are needed for the development of the moral and intellectual qualities. If only through the consciousness of her *ego*, woman is called to take a more important place in the life of nations.

From the dependent that she once was, woman will become the agent required by her times. If she no longer receives from her comrade, as in old Teutonic days, the cuirass, helmet, and sword, that she may fight by his side, she will none the less endeavour to equal him in the field of intellect.

The start which man has gained and still keeps in the realms of Science and Art does not justify him in boasting over the inferiority of woman.

To sum up, woman claims no more than her right to-day when she demands knowledge of all the occupations in which man is employed and reserves for himself; when she desires to exercise her judgment and prove both her skill and taste.

"Whereas in men," says Louis Dimier, "taste, which is a power of the mind, precedes and commands skill, which is organic aptitude; in women, on the other hand, it seems to be skill which determines and commands taste. One might say literally that with a woman the feeling for the beautiful is in her fingers. All women, too, some more and some less, but without exception, make use of their powers of action; but a man cannot rely all his life on the possession of his capacity for judgment."

Yes, woman is, fundamentally, man's equal. Belittled as she has been till recently by conditions which made her a nonentity, she is now, thanks to the spread of education, the mingling of classes, and social changes, becoming a respected worker and a valued being. Born into a new life, she will no longer be the jealous rival of man, but his useful fellow-worker, as she has always been his generous comrade, sharing his joys and sorrows.

THE EQUALISING OF CLASSES BY EDUCATION

THE education which is the progressive adaptation of humanity to the conditions of social life has been, in a general way, so greatly developed by our modern civilisation, that it has, if not created the complete equalisation of the classes, at least brought the aristocracy, the middle classes, and the people together in a common effort towards individual action.

It cannot be denied that a very curious phenomenon exists in the equalisation so far effected, the causes of which are manifold, and amongst which the most noticeable and obvious are the partition of large fortunes, the importance assumed by Labour Syndicalism, and the competition established in all trades and professions.

Scarcely anything remains now of the ancient conditions of nations; the abolition of slavery has transformed the idea of servitude; compulsory education has raised the level of the lower classes, and by this means the first stone of the Socialistic edifice has been laid. But humanity, in attaining to a higher degree of self-consciousness, to a new ideal, has developed a spirit on new lines, and created for itself needs with which the old instincts have nothing to do. Capitalists, manufacturers, merchants, labour leaders, workpeople of all kinds, find themselves arrayed against one another in a new perception of their rights (if not always of their duties), and all, in the light of newly discovered needs, are jostling one another in life in this all-pervading struggle.

The mass of the people, whose one instinct in former times was the bare preservation of life, is on the way to emancipation; the pressure from beneath is mounting like a wave, leaping upward to the social strata where hitherto the monopoly of lucre and jobbery has been jealously held; the workmen's associations, in their war against capital, want themselves to capitalise; members of the working class, with growing improvement in education, are entering the professional field; the middle classes are struggling for the attainment of public offices, and, by an inevitable reaction, the aristocracy, mulcted of some of its ancestral rights and privileges, is turning its eyes towards manufacture and commerce.

This does not mean that the balance has become even, for I am of Jean Lahor's opinion: "The plutocrats may be preparing for the masses of the future a still more crushing yoke, with more falsity and more deadening effect—by the suggestions of the Press, which they have completely in their power—than has ever been the case with aristocracies or autocracies, whose authority had its origin at least in the finer human energies, in a noble desire for power."

It must nevertheless be recognised that, in order that the relations between man and man should no longer be in the hands of those devoid of conscience and feeling, a certain equality, a meeting on common ground for action, has been already established in modern society; if the lower classes have climbed the ladder far enough to attain to that domain which seemed bound to remain in the hands of the higher, the latter, on the other hand, have not hesitated to leave the heights to which class prejudice might have held them, and invade the territory of trade and commerce.

A man of high position will no longer lose caste by becoming the head of a motor factory; a nobleman may take part in commercial enterprise, a prince of the blood sell, in his own name, the products of his vineyards and lands.

It is the same from the point of view of women. As they think more, as they become carried away by the desire to prove their value and the need for individual effort, the middle-class woman is reaching towards higher and higher branches of education. Great ladies, even princesses, do not disdain to draw profit from the industrial arts, from painting and literature.

These new social conditions could not continue but by the spread and improvement of education and the growing sense of justice as understood by Herbert Spencer; that is to say, the responsibility of the individual taken in connection with the need for social co-operation.

Complete equality will never exist; comparative equality must be based on such liberty as, by its exercise, cannot infringe upon the liberties of others.

It must not be forgotten that social harmony is the result of the adjustment of conflicting rights and duties. One has to-day to take into consideration the fact that the humblest artisan is working for the good of society just as is the most famous engineer, the greatest inventor, the noblest writer, or the most celebrated statesman. Therefore, being "morally equal in duty, they are morally equal in rights."

Education, that leveller of castes, dispenser of good, justice, and harmony, is the outcome of the experience of each utilised for the good of all. It should come from ourselves as well as from others, and pass through the way of reason.

"It is through the combined working of all systems of education and hygiene," says the author of *Pessimisme Heroïque*, "it is through the combined energy of all educators and hygienists, that we shall with certainty obtain some day fundamental reforms, and immense progress in the physical, intellectual, and moral life of humanity."

SOCIALISM

OPPOSED to Individualism, Socialism is the idea of social equality in utilising the power, capital, property, labour, etc., of the community. The generalisation of the term means a social compact, a contract between the members of a society.

Born in the eighteenth century, with the theory of good to be shared by the community, Socialism, which should be a united inherent organisation of the social classes, and of the relations of different classes to one another, has become divided into several hostile cliques. Each has its partisans; there is Possibilist Socialism, the Socialism of Marx, Agrarian Socialism, Parliamentary Socialism, English Municipal Socialism, Collectivist Socialism, State Socialism, Christian Socialism, Pulpit Socialism—and more for aught I know.

The very splitting up of the initial idea which aimed at the regulation of the needs of society, proves that it is a very difficult thing to create, in its entirety, a new social machine, capable of satisfying everyone.

It is above all a question, in my opinion, of discovering a form of association which shall defend and protect by its collective force the person and property of each of its members, and through which each one, while united to all, is answerable only to himself (apart from obligations agreed upon), and remains free in his actions.

It should guarantee that no one should be rich enough to take anyone into bondage, and that no one should be poor enough to be compelled to sell himself.

Again, no man should be able to say: "I am hungry, I do not know how to get food: I am cold, I have no means of warming myself: I am homeless, I do not know where to rest my head." No woman must need to make merchandise of herself to escape starvation.

Man being no longer obliged to sell his physical strength or intellect, woman no longer constrained to throw herself into the market, security of life would exist for all, and a sort of equality would be established.

But is not this equality a chimera, and can it exist in practice? Are not abuses inevitable? How can the feelings and duties of everyone be subject to rule, in such a way as to restrict the great as to their wealth and power and the small as to their avarice and covetousness?

Socialism would have to impose a sort of economic equality which would satisfy everyone; so that he who had climbed a few rungs of the social ladder need not envy him who is already at the top. It must, in short, do away with every cause of discontent, envy, and revenge, between the classes who are compelled to have constant dealings with one another. Thus would great social disorder be avoided. But it would be necessary to keep clear of side issues, to take as the base of Socialism the "simplifying of life," always keeping an intellectual and spiritual ideal as the end in view.

"The characteristic of social organisation," says Nicati, "is to be the means of information; a faithful medium between the individuals from whom primarily all activity emanates, and with whom it ends: just as the personal intellect intervenes in the emotional domain, between impressions and the impulses to which they give rise.

"The function of this natural organisation conforms to the religious principles regulating its formation and acts.

"Its ultimate object is to maintain harmony between men, as the intellect maintains harmony amongst the emotions, and to unite them in a common desire for equalisation, balance.

"The doctrine of the cultivation of an intellectual and spiritual ideal, then, may be defined as a natural social organisation having for aim the religious pursuit of good, remembering that we understand by 'religious' that which is consistent with the natural fabric of social relationship; and by 'good' the necessary and natural result of all harmony, balance."

In reality, however, it appears to me that social equilibrium is no better established now than it was before. The weight which tipped one side of the scale is now on the other. The drawbacks of the lack of stability have not yet disappeared.

Why, for instance, should it be thought advantageous that one class, now in possession, be completely despoiled to profit another class, which would then take its place? Whether the inequality existed as from the heights downwards or from the depths upwards, would not the results be exactly the same? Is not the supreme power as dangerous in the hands of the many as in the hands of the privileged?

If it be true that man has a natural right to all that he needs, it is none the less true that his "right" should not exceed the limits of the needful.

In spite of all theories, the social organisation of humanity is not in existence yet, and will not exist so long as society fails to comprehend that its aim is to satisfy the needs of each one, in the order in which they become manifest.

THE WORKING CLASSES

THE part played by the working man in modern society is of extreme importance. This producer of national wealth is the artery which keeps the heart of a country beating.

Jean Lahor says: "The wealth, power, and glory of the country are, in great part, the work of the humblest of her children—of the artisan, the worker, the common soldier, of unknown heroes of whom no one speaks, never will speak; silent whilst in life as they will be when dead."

Lord Avebury, too, says: "It is an interesting illustration of the Unity of Man, and an encouragement to those of us who have no claims to genius, that though, of course, there have been exceptions, still, on the whole, periods of progress have generally been those when a nation has worked and felt together; the advance has been due not entirely to the efforts of a few great men, but of their countrymen generally; not to a single genius, but to a national effort."

Then, since the working man is the great factor in national greatness, it is but just that he should be an object of consideration for the thinkers. This is a truth: the education received by the working man is not consistent with the place which he occupies in the State.

I have in mind, for the children of the working class, schools specially adapted to that class, where the child should be taught his rôle in life as a sort of religion; his employer of the future appearing as a kind of protective deity. The child destined to become an artisan should be made to understand, from the most tender age, not to regard himself as a mere tool, but as the most active element in society. He should be inculcated with pride in his condition, not have his temper embittered and be taught to hate the upper classes, which are, from another point of view, a vital element equally with his own class. The working classes—and this is a point which Socialism and Evolutionism have failed to recognise—should form a majority set apart in the nation, not for the purpose of excluding them from the common good, but, on the contrary, for their advantage, as being the most active and least fortunate.

In all countries which recognise wherein their strength consists, the working man should be the object of constant care on the part of the administration; he should be recompensed according to his merits, and receive help in his needs. The entire health of a country depends so much on that of the working population, that dwellings built in accordance with the most perfect sanitary conditions, public baths and wash-houses, national parks as in America, and institutes where he could educate himself to a higher mental life, should be guaranteed to the working man.

It is very strange that, in democratic countries, the most urgent reforms are generally delayed, that they put off the amelioration of the wretched conditions prevailing amongst the humblest—yet, by numbers and activity, the strongest—class; amelioration which is first carried out in aristocratic countries, such as England.

When French hospitals, for instance, are compared with those in England, Germany, and Russia, a clear idea is gained of the great difference, which does honour to the latter countries.

It is said that the first idea of working men's dwellings originated in France. I admit it; but they only came into existence there after England and Belgium had set the example.

Where in the great French centres will you find the garden cities of England and Germany? Even in the matter of food, from the point of view of price and quality, the French artisan has reason to envy his English neighbour.

The artisan is too cramped by material conditions and constant labour, too much cut off from men superior in mental training to himself; he needs to be taken out of his sordid environment, allowed to acquire property of his own, to give him a taste for home life.

When legislators and rulers, teachers and employers, have taught the working man to recognise his own character and claim respect for his value to society, a thousand rational reforms will spring into being spontaneously.

It seems to me that in manufacturing centres every house should be a temple of fraternity. I will give an illustration: An artisan marries. His wife and he live in a very small house, which, after the birth of their children becomes too cramped for them, and inadequate from a hygienic point of view. Close by, there is an artisan living in a much larger house, as he has had a large family. The children, having grown up, have left their parents, and for this reason the house has become much too large for them. The couple whose family have gone take the little dwelling, and the houseful of children move into the large one. In this way a kindly interchange is made in response to particular requirements; hence, a share of happiness for everyone, and health for all.

Utopia! someone will say. Why? There is really nothing simpler. But then, unfortunately, the simple is always hostile to reason.

DOMESTIC SERVICE

SINCE the disappearance of slavery, domestic service has taken on new forms—variable, oppressive—and now it seems likely to disappear altogether. The terms, Liberty, Equality, Fraternity, misunderstood by some, misconstrued by others, have created great disquietude in society. The servant of former days—the wage-earning man or woman—who formed an integrant part of the family, exists no longer, and those succeeding have changed the old ways and manners to the point of rendering them unacceptable—from the time when *attachment* disappeared before a false conception of *liberty*. So that to-day, amongst people of only moderate means, the lack of servants is becoming a serious problem, although changing fashions and the competition in "special lines of work" secures us assistance in much of our daily business.

We occupy ourselves with workmen's dwellings, have honestly sought to secure better conditions for the poor; why should we not consider the case of those blocks of flats where the closeness of the quarters has become one of the principal hindrances to the "good and loyal service" so much appreciated by our forbears?

Servants in these days consider themselves as employees of a special kind, able to dictate their own terms and exempt from various duties. Their service, continuous and dearly paid, is no longer suitable except in palaces and large private houses.

In these they form a community of their own which is not, each member of it individually, every moment of the day in direct contact with the master and mistress. In such cases as these one scarcely realises the irritating position of servants with regard to their employers, and vice versa.

The question to be considered is that of small establishments and blocks of dwellings in large towns where, for the sake of greater accommodation, the employers' and the servants' quarters are close together, perhaps only divided by glass doors and thin partitions. Now, to ensure respect for the master and mistress in their private life, and willing obedience from the servants, distance in point of fact should be in proportion to distance in point of position and education.

"No great man is a hero to his valet," says the proverb. This proverb is unfortunately true. It describes an evil which has grown to such a degree as to make domestic service in apartments impossible.

In America this question is almost completely settled. In England the example set by the United States is beginning to be followed. The Continent in its turn should evolve some practical expedient for the independence of both employer and employee.

To this end there should be a system of "service by the hour." This will have to be arranged in view of the fear that we may find ourselves servantless. It does not imply that the service now extant will disappear entirely.

Like all innovations, my suggestion will at first alarm some and bring a smile to others; it will seem paradoxical in spite of its simplicity. However, I will explain my idea.

It is not to be denied that we have become servants to our domestics, for they dictate terms on entering our service, and we are compelled to accept their conditions for fear of finding ourselves boycotted and unable to get them at all. In America—I quote typical cases—people have ceased to have their meals at home on Sunday because the *chef* or cook spends that day in the country. In England ladies' maids refuse to wait up for their mistresses' return from evening parties. (I knew an unmarried lady who was compelled to sleep one night dressed as she was because her maid, having locked herself into her room, declined to get up to unfasten her dress for her!) In Germany the servants make it a condition that they shall spend so many evenings at masked balls; in France a weekly or fortnightly "day off" is one of the least inconveniences created by domestic service.

Is it not the truth that in flats, if one had a woman in in case of need, and a sort of watchman to guard against burglars, nothing more would be needed?

"Service by the hour" would have the advantage of providing regular attendance, and the servants themselves would earn more; they would not be obliged to listen to the voice of command from the same master or mistress all day long; they could choose the kind of service they preferred, just as the employer could choose his employees. There would be more freedom on both sides: the one party would work more conscientiously, the other enjoy greater peace of mind. There would be less friction, more justice, all round. In the absence of close proximity there would be no more irritating surveillance, no fear of gossip, no ill-temper over work ill-done or neglected.

If you have a masseur or masseuse, even a "bath attendant," a hairdresser, a manicurist, a packer, a "vacuum cleaner," and a floor polisher, what remains for you to ask of your servants?

If a woman can come and fetch your dresses to be ironed or "freshened," and a man do the same with your coats, and someone else come and polish your boots, is not that all-important?

Companies for "service by the hour" would have to be established in different districts. According to one's needs he would telephone to one of these establishments for a bath attendant, for someone to truss poultry, for housework, etc.

And then how delightful it would be to be alone again, no longer spied upon, to be one's own master—without any servants!

"But the expense!" someone will say. If you calculate what the servants living in your house cost you in one way and another, you will come to the conclusion that there would be less expense for the employer and certain profit for the servants, whose service by the hour would be better paid.

In some of these modern blocks of dwellings there is but one common kitchen. It would be sufficient to mention the hour for meals and the number to be served to ensure regular attendance.

"Service by the hour" would do away with a thousand annoyances, some merely irritating by their frequency, but others serious, as in England, for instance, where the evidence of servants has so much weight in cases of divorce.

With "service by the hour" there would be no more spying, no more mean revenges, no more dishonourable compromises. As the lower classes have shaken off the yoke of their slavery, why should we still be the victims of a new state of things in matters domestic?

There is no perfect happiness without real independence. Let us aim at independence for everyone.

In doing good in a new way the human end in view has not changed. Let us bear in mind that good for all is only found in individual freedom.

INTERNATIONAL SCHOOLS

NOW that the different peoples fraternise over science, commerce, and industry, now that they are jointly liable, in the name of economic relations, now that collective work, free from "national etiquette," is instrumental in producing material and moral progress for all, international schools ought to be founded in the different civilised countries.

These nurseries of the intellect and will would bring pupils together by one single rational system of training; the pupils would be subject to the same examinations; and there would be effected between the different countries an exchange of individualities, destroying race hatred in the idea of rights common to all and the rightful administration of collective communities.

Armed peace, costly as it is for every nation, is a benefit in these modern times. Each nation, by preserving the integrity of its own territory, is more at liberty for intercourse with its neighbours, and for the development of the high ideals which are urging the peoples towards economic unity.

In former times, taking France as an example, the various provinces detested one another, and were at variance through all kinds of conflicting interests. They were separated by the barrier of opposite temperaments, dissimilar customs; each of them preferring to remain a stranger to the rest, though they all spoke the same language. But by means of gradual changes, they were at length drawn together, each province grew to feel a certain oneness of thought with the others, until finally the rigid barriers broke down, and to-day the whole race aims at the training in international feeling of every individual, desiring that future generations, free from too local a patriotism, should attain to what I may call geographical fraternity. For this object nothing would be so valuable as the creation of international schools, by which the tide of different ideas may enter, and thus solve the great problem of comparative education.

Let us imagine similar schools in every country. Young men and girls, sent abroad to follow up the course of study they have begun in their own country, would find the completion of their education in the mental intercourse offered by contact with the boys and girls of the foreign school. They would by this means widen the horizon of their ideas, they would become cosmopolitan without effort, reap such advantages from foreign life as would greatly add to the force of their own personality, and return home with an equipment of sound judgment and self-possession. In addition, they would have learnt the foreign languages so necessary to the pursuit of commerce, manufacture, letters, and the arts.

The young man and the girl thus educated in the idea of world-relationship would hold their own in the circles to which they belonged, and would be certain to do their country good service at an age when, in the ordinary course of things, they might dream of going abroad for the sake of seeing the world, without any ability to profit by that exchange of ideas and comparison of manners which the international school would secure to them just at the impressionable age.

When one considers how useless in most cases, and how invariably costly to parents, travelling is in the case of young men destined for professional or even commercial careers, when undertaken after their education is completed, one must acknowledge the advantage which would result from the exchange between the countries of young, amenable pupils, quick to assimilate all the elements needed for complete training.

Of course each student sent abroad would have professors of his own tongue and race to continue the course of study he was pursuing at home. But from the very fact that they were living in a foreign land, they would be able to learn the new language outside the classroom without any trouble, and become initiated in new ways and ideas, acquiring all sorts of useful knowledge, which would help to mature their minds. So would each one, without losing contact with his own land, profit by the constant recurrence of matters for comparison and analysis.

Sainte-Beuve had conceived the project of such a state of things when, on the eve of the Franco-German War in 1870, he said: "War is being prepared between the two greatest peoples in Europe.... It would be better to found two schools, one in Berlin and one in Paris. The flower of our youth would go and strengthen their minds in the laboratories of Berlin, which are richer than ours; the Prussians would come here and be moulded to our French grace." The real difficulty between nations is that of mutual understanding. Whether it be a question of medicine, manufacture, commerce, or education, there are many efforts made which, in the first instance, are unknown in neighbouring countries, and thereby progress is hindered. By means of international schools, a solution would be found to problems common to all, for instruction would pass from one to another.

In commercial and industrial matters, especially, dealings between one country and another would be carried out more easily, and on a larger scale.

Through uniformity of customs, and harmony in feeling and ideas, brought into play for the good of all, peace would be assured, while rivalry, on which progress depends, would still exist. Autocracy, democracy, imperialism, all would be merged in the common desire for improved conditions.

On the day when harmonious endeavour shall become the rule between people and people, the wealth of the world will increase tenfold, simply through the working of all intelligence for the good of every nation.

THE NECESSITY OF RELIGION, AND ITS INFLUENCE OVER THE PEOPLE

RELIGION is neither a collection of natural laws nor a philosophic dogma. It is higher in dignity than teachers of to-day represent it, and it will be understood if we consider the meaning of the word "religion" as applied to the life of the individual. In the words of Dr. Nicati," ... applied to an individual, it denotes the allied operations of the spirit upon which rests his judgments and actions. As applied to society, it is the symbol of the facts which determine the relations between individuals; it embraces in one common term *the principles of social harmony.*"

In giving us this definition of religion, Dr. Nicati is not considering any creed in particular, but all religions, each of which, taken separately, is a moral code.

The religious idea, which French governments of to-day set aside as useless, is, on the contrary, of obvious utility, primarily for all those whose brains, ill-supplied with mental nourishment, need both spiritual food and also a curb. What a strong restraining force is the fear of eternal punishment; what an encouragement the desire of endless reward!

In vain have all our orators striven, our materialists shown their contempt; it is none the less true that the wiser spirits—men like Littré, Taine, and Renan—have maintained in spite of all that "the people must have a religion, a religion considered purely as an idea inculcating morality."

I will not embark upon the study of the evolution of religions, of the Roman Catholic religion in particular, which, from its origin, remains the moral authority of the Latin peoples. I will simply state that, compulsory education notwithstanding, criminality in France has increased in alarming proportion, whereas in England, as the noble thinker Lord Avebury remarked some time ago, "prisons have had to be closed for want of prisoners."

Let us make no mistake. French criminality is in exact proportion with the lowering of the moral level; the absence of criminality in England comes of the respect shown by our neighbours for all religious sects, provided they use their influence for the development of the religious principle in children— that is to say, the fear of the punishment which comes of wrongdoing, and the hope of the reward which good merits.

Until the moral sense has become thoroughly developed in everyone, religion—that is to say, a preventive training against the passions—will continue necessary.

"We have schools enough of every description," says the author of

L'Education de Soi-Même, "which give us general knowledge and admirable skill in the technique of every branch of human activity; what we need is a school for the making of men." The Church would have remained such a school if the Romanists had not made of their authority a political weapon.

Nevertheless, religious morality dwells in the depths of the mind, and thus it is, according to Maurice de Fleury, "that modern savants who have lost their faith, and cannot believe in human free will, become reconciled ultimately to the teaching given us by the Church."

The rational morality which comes of mental training may be sufficient for the strong, relieving them of a thousand illusions and childish fancies. It remains none the less true, however, that, even amongst those who are past masters in the arts, in science, and politics, there are some who, from an ethical point of view, are spiritual weaklings, needing, in place of the Latin *intelligere*, some creed, hidden or avowed, adapted to their imaginative and imperfectly-controlled brain.

Whatever may be said, the mass of the people has to be considered as an "inferior majority." Apart from it, a "superior minority" stands out; no longer bound by all the old beliefs, but all the same given to an "inner" religion, which is the ethical intelligence whence springs rational morality.

Let us consider the apostle. The inferiority of his followers is manifest, but as soon as these disciples reach a higher level, through the education of their spirit, they in their turn will become apostles, and moral equality will exist in a group which, in its turn again, will win over other groups.

We must then concede to the people a religion which may take the place of the moral law, one giving them the hope of living again in

THE INFANTA EULALIA AND HER TWO SONS
Photograph by Boissonnas & Taponier, Paris.

a better life, affording comfort in affliction, and restraining their cravings. Religious beliefs are but the poetic materialisation of moral truths. By maturing the popular mind, by improved education, the time will come—in some far-distant future—when man will need no other dogma than that natural one which is faith in *himself*, without which he does not (consciously) exist.

On the day when religion shall no longer serve to govern morals, it will be useless. For many it is already a dead letter. That matters nothing in the case of those whose morality, I repeat, is based on reason; but how regrettable when it is a question of persons of inferior intelligence who, without fixed rules, are unable to attain the perception of good and evil!

Amongst certain peoples, a religion was founded by philosophers as long ago as 500 years before Christ. Did not Confucius correct the habits of his country, reform justice, and bring in prosperity, through moral training? Chief authority of a new sect, governed by the idea of rectitude in the life, he organised a state of things which continues yet.

This may happen later on in our Western countries; but until we have replaced the ancient creeds by a moral Ideal impressed upon all minds, it will be necessary to keep up the religious sentiment amongst the people, who have remained hitherto an unconscious force.

THE PRESS

"THE newspaper," says Eugène Tavernier, "is the expression of society." That is a rudimentary truth which has strangely lost its meaning since the Press, whose social rôle was that of an educator, gave itself up to sectarianism, and, in consequence, was no longer able to exercise, for the most part, a really moral influence.

From the fact that the Press sells itself shamelessly to its supporters, it often happens that it attacks the weak and blindly defends the strong, thus making capital out of ostracism and injustice.

Present-day morals have destroyed the original character of the newspaper. In the hands of men more concerned with their personal interests than the good of their country or the pursuit of truth, the Press has sacrificed everything to profit, for money is its object. Newspapers are bazaars where everything is sold, calumny included. And the turmoil of life has made of the journalist a purveyor of sensational news, of paradoxes which falsify the popular judgment, and information as misleading as it is swiftly obtained. The result is that in our democratic times, when everyone claims the right to give expression to his ideas, we see most journalists writing to order and playing the sorry part of impersonal machines.

Since writers worthy of the name found themselves obliged to bow to the will of these dealers in spoilt paper, many of them have refused to write for the daily papers.

Now, as journalistic over-production increases continually, and as the success of many enterprises (based on the exploitation of credulity, the fear of scandal, and excessive advertisement) is almost always in inverse ratio to integrity, hosts of ignorant men,—"men of all work"—shelter themselves behind the newspaper and make a livelihood out of their trash. The day after the Commune, Louis Veuillot said of the Press: "I have been associated with it all my life, and I do not like it. I may say that I hate it; but it belongs to the considerable class of necessary evils. Newspapers have become such a danger that it is necessary to create many. You cannot contend against the Press, except through its multitude. Add flood to flood, and let them drown one another, forming no more than a swamp, or, if you will, a sea. The swamp has its lagoons, the sea its moments of slumber. We will see whether it is possible to build some Venice within it...."

The daring controversialist and uncompromising fighter did not foresee that the Press, far from neutralising itself through its numbers, would, later on, create a State within a State, developed to such an extent, and so imbued with disintegrating principles, that it would become as dangerous to social groups as to individuals.

I shall be told that, since its very modest beginnings, in the time of Louis XIV., the Press was as formidable under the Revolution as later, and that all governments suffered through it. But I reply that in former times the journalist, in spite of many excesses, held his calling sacred, and that his exercise of it found an excuse in his talent and sincerity. It was a time when men of strong opinions fought beneath the same flag; in our own day we often see men pass from one side to the other and defend by turns diametrically opposite views.

In the critic's domain, for instance, it was esteemed an honour to show oneself possessed of a sense of the beautiful. Men like Théophile Gautier, Sainte-Beuve, Paul de Saint-Victor, spared not their personal preferences to pay homage to talent, no matter whence it came.

Art was the first object with spirits like these. To-day, mere talkers, with some dubious interest at their back, are willing to boom any mediocrity who makes it worth their while. Everything is done with an eye to expediency. The independent artist is regarded as an enemy because he will not condescend to pay the paper's price for praise and puffery. It is the same in politics; and whosoever, in commerce or industry, fails to sacrifice to the omnipotent god of advertisement, finds himself checkmated by rivals pushed forward at a great expenditure of bank-notes.

It comes about then that, in a free state, a privileged class, generally recruited from amongst the quasi-intellectual of the "flash-in-the-pan" type, is able to place itself above the law because, in many cases, slander is—or so it appears—a means of instructing or amusing the public.

Not long ago, when the Press was censored, people cried out at the abuse of power; but when it was given freedom to express even destructive opinions, it hastened to turn this freedom into licence. And, in fact, to-day the evil has become so great, through the falsity and baseness of the subject-matter, that the least well-informed reader, seldom though he may look at a paper, knows beforehand the stuff that will be served up to him, whether as regards politics, art, science, or the small change of public scandals.

The intrusion of advertisement, too, is such that the man whose article is published is often the one who pays. In this way, the Lie, in a thousand different forms, is retailed every hour of the day to the poor deluded reading public.

In order that the Press may fill the rôle of educator of the people, leader of the masses, it must adhere to a political, social, and moral ideal, frankly sincere, and with a personal sense of the beautiful.

The opinions of honest, enlightened minds, freed from the snare of time-serving, would be offered to society, instead of such as corrupt individual aspirations or bring a ferment of confusion into the different social spheres.

But, to make that possible, every newspaper should be, first of all, an enterprise possessing considerable capital, supplied by independent shareholders, uncompromising, honourable men, whose fortune would be an element making for success.

Established on a solid and lasting foundation, the Press, in spite of differences of opinion, would become an admirable organ of instruction, such as would waken the intellect, but not satisfy morbid curiosity.

For the spread of thought, selection of the best information from all sources must be considered, not extortion and satisfaction of depraved taste.

When the Press becomes genuine, writers of merit of all kinds will bring to it the tribute of their observation, ideas, and workmanship. When that day comes, the newspaper will be entirely free with regard to political and social groups and private individuals alike, since it will be a common enterprise of good men—men well informed, worthy of their office, and fit for the accomplishment of sound, honest, and praiseworthy work.

MORALITY

MORALITY is a metaphysical quality by the help of which our practical actions are justified, and which in most cases constitutes restraint. Morality is a science, say some; morality is an art, say others; for many idealists it remains a *revanche* of reason, and M. Rodrigues sees in it the will which binds itself and which we bind. "Individual liberty," he says, "if it exists, only plays a part on the second plane; in practice it signifies little when humanity in its entirety is considered. Bound to an organism, and still more to society, the psychological or moral consciousness, when it draws inspiration from within itself, finds there in effect what its *milieu* has placed there. It expresses a system of representations, to the forming of which it has in itself contributed but a small part.... Morality, too, has undergone an evolution parallel in all points to that of science."

Yes, truly, morality, like everything which touches on conduct, social laws, rites, traditions, ancestral prejudices, the need of freedom, the right of the individual, undergoes continual evolution according to the conditions of a community. We are to-day far from the morality which, according to Kant, is legislation on the part of the reasonable being, enjoining upon all persons the same duties.

According to the morality of Epictetus, resting on the idea of liberty, "man may free himself of all dependence with regard to other men and to Nature, and raise himself to absolute freedom, distinguishing between the things which rest on him and those which do not, and despising the latter as immaterial"; according to the ethics of Epicurus, pleasure is the sovereign good of man, and all our efforts should tend towards its attainment, provided that pleasure consist as much of the satisfaction of the heart and mind as of the senses, but modern morality has become sectarian, and differs according to class.

The principle of *bourgeois* morality is to preserve the unity of the community without any consideration for the liberty of the individual; the *bourgeois* family being a sort of commercial association, it confines its morality to the idea of a duty which is, above all, the protection of the interests of the community. It is a morality which is quite beside the point, and which has no intrinsic value.

The principle of aristocratic morality is to preserve for the glory of its escutcheon all the splendour it deems requisite. It does not trouble itself as to the means by which that escutcheon gains in radiance, because it has made a virtue of its pride. The superadded adornments trouble it with no pangs of conscience, because for it duty consists in the integrity of appearances. This morality is not, in the main, more false in conception than that of the *bourgeois*; it is the guardian of appanage as the other is the guardian of selfish interests.

The morality of Courts consists in preserving tradition intact, and it does not hesitate to sacrifice individuals to the Cause which is one, unchangeable, and imperative. It is thus a morality extraordinary, having authority above right and outside duty.

But whatsoever constitutes the quality deemed essential, whether it be the commercial and industrial stability of the *bourgeois*, the true or false splendour of the nobleman's escutcheon, or the more or less artificial halo of the Court, it is none the less true that class morality is daily obliged to yield to circumstances and bend to conditions.

Being one of the manifestations of human action, morality is necessarily subject to the law of living according to such and such an epoch. It has to adapt itself to change. For this reason personal interest, selfishness, pride of birth, and the idea of being above humanity must all, in spite of their rules, conform to new conceptions of altruism and idealism, for there is no moral finality.

To speak truly, every individual bears the moral sense within himself, but he has to remember that the sanction of moral judgment is one of the most important factors of civilisation and progress, and cannot be dissociated to-day from the scientific element.

Nothing leads men more astray than to let them believe that certain persons or certain things injurious to society are desirable.

The personal interest of the merchant is not adapted to the artisan's life conditions; an escutcheon is not a thing to be coveted by the worker; and the right called "Divine" diminishes in no degree the right of a people. On the contrary, class morality is hostile to the new moral ideas answering to new social needs; this is the reason why its value has depreciated, because humanity is making a constant effort towards an ideal which it creates and changes according to the difficulties of the way, and because the straight road leads to righteousness.

PUBLIC OPINION

"IT is easy, in the world, to live after the world's opinion," says Emerson; "it is easy in solitude to live after our own; but the great man is he who, in the midst of a crowd, keeps with perfect sweetness the independence of solitude."

In this logical rounding of his thought, the master has given us a rule of conduct based on self-confidence, the result of vigorous mind-training and the exchange of opinion.

Every slave to public opinion lives irresponsibly, because he fails to possess his own soul, is incapable of inward control, and unable to arrive at an independent view.

To be checked by public opinion means the abandonment of mental effort, the surrender of the *"I"*; it means resigning oneself to become mere reflection, a nonentity.

Not to everyone is it given to be able to brave public opinion; only a few have the force to throw off social conventions.

One of the conditions permitting of contempt of public opinion is to have no need of anyone, both from the point of view of material existence and of moral status. I am not speaking of those on whom fortune has smiled from their birth, but of the great majority who, lacking firmness of character and matured personality, obey blindly as circumstances dictate.

What is public opinion if not a collection of incongruous judgments turned to general use, rules followed from force of custom, hypocritical virtues, lies in disguise? And why should not I hold to my own private view, in spite of current opinion, if, in the consciousness of pure intention, wisdom in action, I show forth in my conduct the precepts guiding my life?

Is public opinion responsible for my mistakes? Am I less good, less just, less loyal because unshackled by imitation, lack of originality, and affectation? Why, then, should I deprive myself of honest happiness for fear opinion should turn against me?

Why should I bow to circumstances which I have not created? Why, once more, should I not be myself?

The desire for general approbation is a sign of weakness, a defect of the mind and conscience. It is allowing someone else to know your duty better than yourself and force upon you preconceived notions, neutral, limited ideas of action and thought.

Woe betide those who fall under such influence. They resign themselves to an existence of mental wretchedness, painfully dragging out their days in hesitation and spiritual cowardice, never able to realise that public opinion has no moral worth, but, though varying according to country, conditions, and training, is nevertheless intolerant, mean, and arbitrary everywhere.

The careless judgments given by public opinion always assume too much, and are not the result of harmony between conduct and principle on the part of those who form them. We should show ourselves fearlessly for what we are, speak our own language with sincerity, express our thought directly to-day, to-morrow, the day after to-morrow. Even if we contradict ourselves on certain points, that is but a proof of our readiness to be better, more just. To be true to oneself is the great secret of personality, and prevents all fear of our neighbour.

A matured, steadfast spirit, a sound brain given to meditation, a conscience sharpened by training, constitute a character which can afford to despise public opinion, and command an entrance for itself to all the paths of life.

This state of individualism does not imply systematic opposition to the customs of the day. It is not hostile to society, but it enables one to shake off the yoke of public opinion, and assert with sweetness his personality.

PREJUDICES

PREJUDICES, or preconceived opinions adopted at random, subsist indefinitely. Like creeds, they are a malady of weak minds which unquestioningly accept relative moral laws, formulas which the reason cannot admit, and errors which live and propagate faster than truths.

Those are persons without judgment or discernment who profess to do as all the world does, because they have not the force to form an independent opinion, undergo the discipline of thought, examine their own actions, and confess the absurdity of their own weaknesses.

It is not to be denied that minds trained by mental gymnastics have little to say to prejudices. Their judgment being independent, they require perfect freedom of action, and they cannot permit a host of trifling considerations to hinder them in their way of living and thinking.

Prejudices—a form of mental aberration—are a standard by which the least intelligent claim to estimate the capacities of others. And those prejudices which proceed from stupid customs, absurd fears, silly superstitions, have led to the most annoying assertions.

It is a matter of general belief, for instance, that the number 13 is unlucky, that the song of a black bird is a sign of death, that three lights bring misfortune; and the belief is not less general that persons of high birth are inevitably lacking in great intelligence. It has been decided once for all that they are unfit for intellectual work, and capable only of being pleasant company, as superficial as useless. If these persons take up any intellectual pursuit, be it the publishing of books, or devoting themselves to art, they are misjudged, there is an outcry at the unreality, the gross impossibility; for it has been decided that high birth should be a patent of incapacity.

Prejudice thus destroys beforehand the proof of intelligence and tarnishes reputation. At the same time, in the form of conventional, generally-received opinions, it overawes timid spirits.

It is in frivolous society that prejudices are most ineradicable. They creep into conversation, obtrude themselves in all their bareness and ugliness into the midst of chatter and compliments.

Even if some strong personality appears, and disposes of some prejudice, it shoots up again directly the disturber is gone. Born of folly and fear, prejudices are parasitic plants whose roots are in the brain, and which are transmitted, like an heirloom of ignorance, from one century to another.

Prejudices, so numerous in these days, fall foul of everything: art, science, law, the liberty of the individual, conscience, truth.

Is it not regarded as a fact, in certain circles, that the Jew is incapable of fine intelligence? Now, for the last twenty-five years dramatic art has given the lie flatly to such an assertion. Has not the man of science, in spite of every proof of his capacity, been attacked by prejudiced people who see in him an insulter of the Divinity?

Is not the education of the people regarded in many cases as a danger to society? Is not the creation of new laws, designed for ensuring the rights of all, considered monstrous? Now that human consciousness has developed, now that the will is being trained to righteousness, now that personal responsibility has entered our life conditions, and moral education has become rational, it is really strange to see people who claim intelligence, and who pass for well informed, accept the absurd prejudices in vogue.

Women, it must be said, are for the most part hostile to progress. Through heredity, through habit, they take up prejudices with a fervour that deludes their superficial minds. Two pernicious elements, jealousy and envy, conduce to this. Prejudiced men are no less dangerous, for, being incapable of thinking for themselves, and not willing to think through others, they are unable to correct their own errors.

My conclusion is that all slaves of prejudice should be compelled to live together, separated from the living and thinking world, until the day comes when, being no longer satisfied with themselves, they will begin to be endurable to others.

JUDGMENT

JUDGMENT is the faculty of discrimination in ideas, of establishing a connection between the state of our conscience and reality. But as conscience varies according to the nature of social situations, it does not seem possible to apply a fixed rule to judgment, though it always requires affirmation. Whatever be the degree of judgment one possesses, one cannot exercise it in the case of others without first applying the precept, "Know thyself"—an ancient utterance which has lost a little in value since it has been handed down, without sincerity, from generation to generation. This precept is, nevertheless, held in honour by the finer spirits, for it is obvious that the appeal to our conscience should be placed above all others. Without this, as Nicati says, "the man who forgets to examine himself, and whose personality is effaced thereby, counts for less than the inert matter whose very resistance constitutes personality."

He who lives according to his conscience, and after his own moral laws, may be satisfied. When he comes to judge himself, he knows that his life has been passed in the observance of his own personal principles.

We must, then, seek in ourselves a standard of judgment, remembering the beautiful words of Thomas à Kempis: "Turn thine eyes unto thyself, and beware thou judge not the deeds of other men. In judging of others, a man laboureth in vain, often erreth, and easily sinneth; but in judging and discussing of himself, he always laboureth fruitfully."

Nevertheless, in self-judgment, it is right to apply severely to ourselves the rules of reason and virtue so far as our own nature permits. It is to be noted that witty people, or those with a good memory, are not the most capable of clear and profound judgment. Assimilation is prejudicial to reflection; memory is not thought.

When our own ideas are clear to us, we shall not judge others without due study of their reasons for what they do, the motives by which they have been governed, the circumstances which may have influenced their estimate of good and evil. Thus our attitude will be more kindly, and we shall avoid all the evils springing from injustice and false judgment.

Our own conscience is not always in the ascendant. We often yield to weakness, and it is only just that our knowledge of the limitations of the human will should move us to indulgence towards our fellow-men.

Such indulgence consists in recognising our own weaknesses, and in not condemning others for what we consider their errors.

The first condition for judging clearly and soundly is the constant attention to our mental life, acknowledging to ourselves our own changes of mood, ceaselessly fighting the enemy within us.

From the altruistic point of view, we should picture to ourselves the person to be judged in the circumstances which have prompted his action—difficult though it be to perceive the differences between characters and shades of feeling—according to the numberless cases in which such action takes place. This is the reason why historians, in the act of composition, so often pass false judgments on the past. In their desire to make the characters live again, to call up vanished scenes, they become partisans, loving or hating those whom they have never known. Purely in deference to their own opinion, they fail in tolerance and indulgence. They do not estimate the worth of men of past days according to the moral tone of the epoch in which they lived; they judge of a society as a whole in the light of isolated documents, so that the men of vanished ages cut but a poor figure in their eyes to-day.

Now, the truth is that men are no greater now than in the other ages of the world. Removed from our own time by twenty-two centuries, the heroes of Plutarch remain as noble as our heroes of to-day; and in the domain of science, religion, and philosophy we have but changed names without changing at all in judgment and logic, without modifying the conditions of happiness or the outward signs of courage, and without developing the human "*I.*"

THE FEAR OF RIDICULE

THE fear of ridicule is a terrible and powerful weapon in the eyes of many people. Cleverly handled by those who are slaves to custom and fashion, this fear of ridicule often prevents our obeying our true feelings, and leads us to act against our own interests.

Many persons whose social position is uncertain, or whose moral force is but little developed, have their days embittered by the thought of "what people will say."

If these persons could only comprehend that nothing which is *simple* and *sincere* can be ridiculous, if vanity and amour-propre would permit them to understand that criticism is inevitable, that it increases self-confidence in well-balanced people, and in many cases helps us towards the end we wish to attain, they would not only cease to fear the observation of others, but no longer wish to suppress the personality of a neighbour.

They would say with Emerson: "That which I ought to do concerns my personality, and not what people think I ought to do."

They would remember these words of La Bruyère's: "'We must do as others do' is a suspicious maxim, signifying nearly always 'We must do wrong' as soon as it extends beyond the purely outward things which result in nothing, and which depend upon custom, fashion, and manners."

A modern thinker, under the veil of anonymity, remarks wittily: "If one wishes to be in good society, even with those who are not of it, need one give up being oneself? Good society, pushed to this excess, is only folly and trickery. What on earth have you done with your amour-propre on these occasions? Dare to say what you think, if you *do* think." I add to this: Dare to do what seems to you good, useful, and sensible; flee preconceived opinions, do not let yourself be influenced by the ideas of others, keep your independence in the face of new suggestions, convince yourself of your own value, call your perceptions into play, suppress your self-love—in a word, get rid of the fear of ridicule, which, carried to excess by people, has spoilt fine careers, ruined the noblest hopes; destroyed for one his dawning happiness, for another possible fortune. Why this mean respect for *what is done*, and absurd fear of *what is not done*? Why this foolish imitation, this holding back of your real self? Why don't you eat and drink what you like? Why spoil your behaviour in public by hypocrisy? Where is the sense of this perpetual dressing up of things which ties you down to convention not in keeping with the real impulses of your heart and mind?

There is so much fear of ridicule in the world that one may see a man miss an interview which might be morally or materially useful to him because he is afraid to appear unfashionably dressed, because he has not the latest hat, or the shoes which snobbism has decreed the correct thing.

Women, in whom the fear of ridicule is so strong, so intimately linked with the taste of the moment, will willingly risk their health rather than go down in the estimation of others.

If, for example, fashion decrees thin summer clothing, a woman will brave bronchitis and the after-effects to wear it; and she acts in a similar spirit with regard to winter fashions, because it is not the right thing to think with one's own mind, feel with one's own heart, or live according to one's own means, nerves, or senses!

This passive life by rule is a curious thing, and Montaigne was right—for folly belongs to all periods—in thus speaking of it for his own epoch: "In some sort all the opinions we have are taken on authority, or on credit, ... Everyone is richer than he thinks, but we go about borrowing and seeking; it suits us better to make use of others than of ourselves.... We neither essay nor know our own faculties; we invest in those of others, and let our own lie idle...."

Yes, truly, the fear of ridicule is one of the worst shortcomings of education, for it destroys character, leads all our impulses towards folly, and often incites to irreparable wrong.

How many marriages which might have been happy are prevented because of difference in fortune, age, or birth! The fear of ridicule brings a disintegrating element even into the quest after happiness, which is a law of Nature.

It is the same with the fear of ridicule as with morality; everyone should base his individual action on some good to be gained, get rid of all constraint—in a word, be himself without depending on custom and outward circumstances; preserving the balance between his conscience, trained by experience and reason, and his personal faculties.

MORAL COURAGE

MORAL courage is that energy of character which leads us to confess and uphold what we think and believe. This quality, one of the rarest in man, is nevertheless indispensable to whomsoever uses his faculties in any public capacity, whether he be a statesman, a soldier, an artist, or a writer; that is to say, everyone who has to take responsibility, making nothing of opinion or criticism.

I have often heard it said that moral courage corresponds to physical development. That is true, provided that the physical development be attended by good health. We often see men insignificant in appearance gifted with moral courage which athletes lack. It is because, in spite of their physical slightness, these men possess health so robust as to save them from mental weakness and give them perfect balance.

But there is something besides. Although there is still much to learn about character, it is certain that we can cultivate the moral courage which springs from instinct and temperament by the choice of our own ideas and actions.

Never has the need of character-forming made itself felt so much as in our days. Character is becoming rare because intellects are in disorder. Dilettantism kills reason, æstheticism strays without direction through the mind, ready-made opinions take the place of thought, and the caprice of the moment serves for moral or material interests and weakens the will.

The sign of the individual, the dominant feature of his personality, is character, and character gives birth to moral courage. Dr. Ferrand says: "Character assumes considerable importance in the life of the individual and in the life of all the natural or social groups which individuals form amongst themselves; it is, accordingly to Smiles, one of the greatest motive powers in the world. By the unity of direction which he impresses upon all his actions, the man of character is not only master of himself, though that is much, but he bears naturally upon the activity of others, and

THE INFANTA EULALIA AND HER TWO SONS
Photograph by Boissonnas & Taponier, Paris.

draws them after him, as a mighty ship draws into its track all the craft it encounters in its course."

There is yet another consideration. By the side of the intellectual element, by which we estimate our thoughts and actions, there is feeling; that is, the sensibility which modifies the judgment and enlightens the deep thought determining our responsibility. He who obeys feeling, when the latter is not subject to the control of thought, commits many errors of judgment and lets himself be guided by moods which may lead him into injustice and breach of trust. Let us not forget that justice is truth applied to the things of life. Now, it is precisely the absence of this idea of justice in the modern consciousness which brings us daily face to face with a sort of failure in moral courage, both as regards attack and defence.

Politics during the last few years have furnished us with sad examples of this weakness; letters and the arts have also given us instances, and they are very regrettable from every point of view.

Literary and musical criticism is to be noted particularly for many lapses; science itself is not exempt from dealings which reason disapproves, and it is not even to lack of education that this shortcoming is due. And we find this lack of moral courage in communities which have blindly turned liberty to a revolting slavery.

Consider parliaments, study castes, look closely at groups of individuals served by opinion, and you will see that real characters worthy to inspire the good, the beautiful, and the true are overwhelmed in the host occupied in ruining the popular conscience.

Individual moral courage is what makes the greatness of a people. This form of courage tends to disappear more and more, because everyone is losing the idea of his own responsibility, and, inspired by selfishness, troubles himself not at all to make justice and virtue respected.

How few men we see use their authority to repair an error, punish a lie or any villainy whatsoever! Weakness, hesitation, doubt, lack of initiative, indifference, have taken the place of moral courage, and that through the lack of character-training. As Emerson says: "No change of circumstances can repair a fault of character.... What have I gained ... if I quake at opinion, the public opinion, as we call it; or at the threat of assault, or contumely, or bad neighbours, or poverty, or mutilation, or at the rumour of revolution, or of murder? If I quake, what matters it what I quake at?"

Each of us, then, should in his own sphere of action become conscious of what is right, and not hesitate to struggle, even to the detriment of his private interests, against all false judgment attacking honour, every opinion concealing baseness, every action which is an insult to reason and to the liberty of the individual.

TRADITIONS

TRADITION is a link of the present with the past, the transmitting of legendary memories from century to century—memories based on real facts, exaggerated or deformed by the popular mind in quest of the ideal.

Traditions of pagan or religious essence are multiform. In most cases they denote blind reverence, unconscious veneration for creeds turned into customs; they are a sign of the passivity of the human mind, whose chief weakness is superstition.

Whether as regards action or thought, tradition appeals to the special organisation of certain temperaments of a primitive order, or which are purely dogmatic.

The desire to maintain tradition implies uncontrolled deference to custom together with the need for moral or sectarian order, and for this reason it is detrimental to the gradual change of thought on which progress depends.

In all ages of the world, since the period when oral narration was handed down from generation to generation, traditions have been accepted as truths. Now, that which was truth at the exact moment when a certain thing occurred is no longer truth after a long lapse of time, because of changes with regard to the original fact and the false interpretations put upon it by the crowd.

Locke says with much truth: "A man worthy of belief bringing testimony of a thing known to him affords a good proof; but if another man equally worthy of credence testifies on the report of that man, his witness is weaker; while that of a third who attests a hearsay is still less to be considered; so that in truths that come by tradition each degree of remoteness from the original source weakens the force of the proof; and in proportion as a tradition passes successively through more hands, it has ever less force and evidence."

This is the reason that traditions, from whatsoever source they come, constitute false propositions all the more dangerous because to many they appear incontestable. After Christianity was established, tradition had all the value of an idealism capable of inspiring individual action; under different aspects it induced respect for great moral acts, linked up more closely familiar ties (the festival of Christmas—Noël or Yule—is a case in point), it cemented friendships, gave value to the idea of good rewarded and evil punished, created an atmosphere of justice and fear, inward joy and hope.

But with time, as the sense of personality developed and social friction became more frequent, it came about that traditions were divided into different camps, some being simply a consolation for the afflicted, others becoming authoritative in the hands of priests and judges. Centuries passed, changing names and beliefs, modifying desires and interests; then tradition weakened and altered in character and significance.

Even in our own day, however, many ancient traditions are rigorously observed both in town and country. Still, as the social movement has become more accentuated, more conscious, they have so weakened that they are more like a list of festival days in the calendar than anything else. In spite of castes which, by holding together, still maintained tradition, the evolution of the masses gradually brought about, through force of circumstances, the destruction of such as was useless. This is good because, I repeat, tradition is hostile to progress in that it makes error in the guise of custom predominate over science and altruistic duty.

The weakening of pagan or religious traditions is very noticeable to-day. For instance, the observance of the anniversaries of the dead is falling into desuetude. One scarcely sees, except in the Latin countries where civilisation is backward, the relatives in deep black coming at a fixed date to mourn their dead from midnight to midnight. This traditional custom, besides, has lost so much of its ancient solemnity that the mourners do not hesitate to dance and feast directly the time of forced grief is over. This anomaly is frequent in Spain nowadays. As soon as the "accessories" of the tradition disappear, the tradition itself will vanish in its turn.

Go through the villages and you will note the disappearance of numbers of customs to which the inhabitants were slaves not long ago. Where, to-day, are the processions in the open fields, the patronal festivals, the inquiries at fountains, all the traces of ancient beliefs? Where, as in Rome in times past, is the lachrymatory, in which, on days of funerals, everyone collected his tears?

Man, as he grows conscious of his forces, his rights, throws off a thousand obligations created for the most part by fear, that slayer of the will.

So it is that lovers of tradition, still struggling to maintain obscurantism amongst the simple and poor, and authoritative creeds amongst the other classes, are attempting a work as difficult as it is inauspicious. Their task will soon be unavailing, for the masses are the true supporters or destroyers of tradition, and the masses will no longer keep up worthless traditions the object of which is to oppose their enlightenment and their interests.

CRITICISM

CRITICISM, taken in its general sense, is the free exercise of judgment. Whether it be a question of literary, artistic, or intellectual analysis—that is to say, the observation of the beautiful—or of philosophy, history, or philology, experimental or exact sciences, criticism is necessary, as it shows the value of a conception and realisation. Now this criticism is a source of dread in many circles, fettering the actions of many, and paralysing their wills. As against this evil, which is too frequent nowadays, some reaction is needed; for it is not more unwise to seek criticism as a means of advertisement than to make a bugbear of it or shun it for fear of wounded pride.

I say that the expression of an opinion contrary to our own should not, logically speaking, slacken our efforts, suppress our inclinations, or lead us to hypocritical actions.

It helps us greatly against the fear of others' criticism to force ourselves to become our own critics—a very difficult matter, but exceedingly profitable.

By this kind of exercise of the conscience we arrive more easily at an understanding of the criticism we receive from without, and learn to despise the envy and jealousy by which it may be actuated. So, too, we may benefit by the lessons derived from an honest analysis of our own qualities and defects.

Criticism, if sincere, only expresses what it perceives clearly. For it, personal evidence becomes a guarantee.

But, it will be said, criticism is often the expression of severity. Would you have it the expression of culpable indulgence? When severe, it is an element tending towards self-control; too indulgent, it can only foster vanity. The mission of criticism is not to determine our actions; its duty is to judge them to its own satisfaction.

For instance, it is obvious that, in the case of writers, painters, and musicians, the critic has only to consider the question of taste. If he attempts to destroy what is estimable, he dishonours himself, and so becomes useless; if he accords praise, he can only express it according to his personal judgment.

Within ourselves, the critic of our reasoned or impulsive actions is a spectator looking through the windows of our soul, seeing our motives as it were from between the curtains, and for this reason unable to judge clearly. This critic, as we know by sad experience, is not worth listening to.

We shall be safe, however, when we are conscious of the fineness of our achievements, the purity of our intentions, the dignity of our actions, or the mere joy of our feelings, in permitting criticism to do its work and pursuing our way.

This does not imply that it always answers to treat judicious criticism with contempt.

Just as in politics, opposition is necessary for the best public administration of the party in power, so in private life criticism is an element in that emulation which aids us to attain the end we have in view.

THE DANGER OF EXCESSIVE ANALYSIS

IF there exist but few people who have any taste for synthesis, there are many whose passion for analysis is pushed to the most exaggerated limits.

Certainly, a continual examination of conscience is necessary if we would escape both useless scruples and irrational desires; certainly, it is good to look squarely in the face the near or remote consequences of our actions; certainly, too, we ought to investigate in all sincerity the secret motives which cause our acts, so that we may correct our errors, taste the delight of well-doing, profit by the lessons of the past, and, in short, satisfy the needs of ethical culture.

By criticising ourselves, looking inward, training ourselves in abstract ideas, and submitting to the laws of mental attainment, we gain the moral instinct which everyone should possess.

If, on the other hand, pushed by the desire to be strictly honest, we analyse our actions too minutely, we shall disturb the balance of our judgment; while, if we thus investigate the doings of others, we shall begin to depreciate great or noble actions until, by our false interpretation of them, we lose the power to perceive them at all.

If, taking separately each idea comprised in an abstract general notion, each small fact composing some important action, we study such parts analytically, we falsify their quality and quantity just as we falsify forms observed through a magnifying glass. Trifling defects appear enlarged and developed, and injure the beauty of the whole—the harmony of a great idea, or the carrying out of an enterprise. I do not deny that, to become morally great, we must imagine great things; I know well that an action is only of value in proportion to the virtue of the end in view; I am not ignorant of the fact that it is useful to look inward; but I do say that too severe analysis applied to all our actions, or those of others, as much in the case of trifles as in serious matters, makes one unjust to his neighbour and himself, and always tends to impair the workings of the intellect.

By scrutinising all the motives by which action has been determined, you rob that action either of its beauty or its goodness, and you will suffer doubly—both with regard to yourself and others.

For instance, you say to yourself: "Was I right in doing such a kind action?" And if, in the process of deduction (whether you consider the service useless because rendered to one not perfectly worthy of it, or doubt beforehand of the gratitude due to you), you come to regret the altruistic impulse on which you acted, you will at once destroy all the pleasure you felt, and you will do wrong to the person you have befriended by a coldness of feeling he has not deserved. Examples might be cited indefinitely. By this excessive analysis you can transform an act of self-sacrifice into an act of narrow egotism, an excuse into a meanness, a certainty into an hypothesis, or a sincere affection into a selfish pretence. This, as regards others; in regard to oneself, the result will be great hesitation, confusion of ideas, disturbance of thought, continual uneasiness and dissatisfaction.

I have only spoken of the misuse of analysis, for its normal use in the mental life is useful, especially when the whole of the facts of the case in point are taken into consideration, as they should never fail to be.

Paulhan says: "Though analysis is to some extent necessary to all mental action, it assumes supreme importance in certain operations of the spirit. They are those which we see govern analytical minds lacking the power of synthesis. Observation, the habit of noticing details, rests mainly on analysis, and the same is true of the faculty of comprehending the thoughts of others. Memory, too, especially the organised memory which implies the discrimination between impressions and ideas, is also founded on analysis; the same with criticism, the detailed and reasoned appreciation of a work of art, science, or philosophy. Certain qualities of the mind and even the character, again, imply the faculty of analysis in a high degree; for instance, finesse, delicacy, the spirit of scepticism and the love of detail."

Granting all this, I say that excessive analysis is a danger. To be useful, it must have the qualities of precision, delicacy, and depth, and not those of vagueness, violence, and exaggeration.

THE LAW OF COMPENSATION

WHEN Azaïs, at the beginning of the nineteenth century, published his *Compensations dans les Destinées Humaines*, he stated, in principle, this proposition: "The lot of man, considered in its entirety, is the work of the whole of Nature, and all men are equal by their lot."

La Rochefoucauld, long before him, said: "Whatsoever difference may appear between fortunes, there is, nevertheless, a certain balancing of good and evil which makes them equal."

One sees that compensation is a principle of optimism. Whatever may be advanced by the many makers of systems, this law is manifest amongst all peoples as in all individuals, including those who, whilst ceaselessly regretting their ill-fortune, yet taste, relatively, a little of the sweetness of compensation if only in their own prudence and courage.

The law of compensation is certainly the most consoling that we can desire, and to it all human morality is allied.

It is surprising to read these words from the pen of Droz: "The absurd system of compensation, would have, as its result, apathy, contempt for the troubles of others, and the most odious selfishness." The conviction that sorrow has joy on the reverse side, that suffering makes health prized, that regret is doubled by memory, is no hindrance, that I am aware of, to sharing in the griefs and joys of others.

Altruism, besides, which so many teachers practise so ill, is nothing but the perfection of egoism, paradoxical though this may seem to some.

Nietzsche says: "An altruistic morality, a morality in which selfishness dies, is in every case a bad sign. It is so in the case both of individuals and peoples. We lose the best of our instincts when we begin to fail in egoism. The instinctive selection of that which is detrimental to us, the allowing ourselves to be deluded by 'disinterested' motives, is almost the doctrine of *decadence*."

Without going so far as this master of aphorisms, I say that egoism cannot be opposed to altruism, and that the law of compensation does not create reprehensible egoism—that which consists in thinking of oneself only.

Egoism is useful; it is legitimate when it is an action only concerning ourselves and not prejudicial to others. Of this very egoism comes the moral philosophy of compensation, for the quest of happiness is fundamentally the utmost possible mitigation of evil. Let us hear Emerson: "The same dualism underlies the nature and condition of man. Every excess causes a defect; every defect an excess. Every sweet hath its sour; every evil its good. Every faculty which is a receiver of pleasure has an equal penalty put on its abuse.

It is to answer for its moderation with its life. For every grain of wit there is a grain of folly. For everything you have missed you have gained something else; and for everything you gain you lose something."

It is quite certain that the ambitious man who has gained power and who rules a nation has greater responsibilities than the humble artisan. If he break his promises, if his ideas be not realised, he falls, betrayed, despised, abandoned, while the worker goes on with his task with the satisfaction of duty done. In what concerns the real blessings of man all are alike, taking into consideration class and accompanying circumstances. Wealth cannot prevent death from entering the dwelling; poverty knows the joys of the deepest affection. When a great tyrant arises, the strength of the people to resist increases tenfold; punishment lies close to reward. All conditions are in the human soul. To come under the law of compensation is not to be able to escape one's destiny. The acceptance of evil is the assurance of better things through moral effort. The sensualist suffers through his sensations, the sage rejoices in his wisdom. And everywhere is the soul untiring in the quest of what is good, right, and just. It must have life, though it find life amid the worst misery and the lowest of decay.

For this reason the doctrine of Nemesis is eternal. Every action entails reaction, every sorrow and every joy has its degree in the social scale. The man born rich will suffer more through the misery created by ruin than the poor man whose pockets are always empty. One has nothing to envy the other.

"No man had ever a point of pride that was not injurious to him," says Burke. Fear is the punishment of the unjust. The law of compensation is not that of indifference, for, without the moral sense no excuse is found for error, and there is no satisfaction for a fault grown to a habit.

The belief that a grief will be compensated for by a joy will bring no comfort to the spirit, unless the soul assert itself.

We must in every circumstance assert our "I," keep our conscience on the alert, and look to the nature of our own soul to find compensation for inequality of condition. Let the rich man receive the rich; if I am poor, I will take the poor to my heart.

The love of those above me in fortune and power cannot prevent my love from being what it is; my little sorrows and joys will be neither heavier nor less sweet than the griefs of the rich and their triumphs.

Regarded so, the law of compensation is the finest element in the formation of character.

THE AUTHOR AND HER BOOK

THE foregoing pages must inevitably arouse in the reader's mind a curiosity to know more of the author. It is rarely that a princess of Royal blood sets down in writing, and publishes for all the world to read, her personal views of the established institutions of civilisation and the inherent virtues and vices of mankind, and when those views prove to be the very antithesis of what might be expected from one born and bred in the restricted atmosphere of a European Court, curiosity is still further whetted. The broad socialism—using the word in its widest sense—which characterises the Infanta Eulalia's views of life would have been a surprising product of any Royal House; emanating as it does from the Royal House of Spain it is no less than amazing, as King Alfonso's action in regard to this book (which we deal with later) further shows.

A knowledge of the Infanta's life will enable the discerning reader to detect the influences which have laid open her mind to liberal and democratic ideas, fostered her remarkable independence of thought, and given her the moral courage to express her well considered opinions. She was little more than a baby when the revolution which dethroned her mother, Isabella II., sent them both in exile to France. It was in September, 1868, that Queen Isabella, who had been living in a fool's paradise at Lequetio, on the Biscay coast, enjoying sea-bathing, at last realised that Spain would no longer tolerate her rule, for Admiral Topete, in command of the squadron in Cadiz Bay, hoisted the flag of revolt. All Spain was waiting for this spark, which kindled a fire not easily to be extinguished. The Battle of Alceola followed, when Serrano, representing the Revolution, defeated Pavia, who defended the tottering regime, and the road to Madrid was open. Isabella heard of Alceola five days after the fight, i.e. on the 29th September, 1868. Soon after, the news reached her of the unanimous rising of Madrid, the deposition of the Bourbon dynasty, and the formation of a provisional Government. She realised then that there was nothing left for her to do but to cross the frontier into France. The abdication of her throne in favour of her son Alfonso took place some years later. In France she first resided at the Castle of Pau, then in Paris, in the Pavillon de Rohan, an annexe of the Tuileries fronting on the Rue de Rivoli. During the winter of 1868-1869 she bought a house in the Avenue du Roi de Rome (now the Avenue Kléber), named it the Palace of Castile, and dwelt there till her death.

At that time, the authoress of "The Thread of Life," the Infanta Marie-Eulalie-Françoise d'Assise-Marguerite-Roberte-Isabelle-Françoise de Paule-Christine-Marie de la Piedad, to mention a few of the many names bestowed on her, was three and a half years old, having been born in Madrid on the

12th of February, 1864. Two and a half years later, the little girl's education was entrusted to the Ladies of the Sacred Heart, whose famed institution in Paris stood in the Rue de Varenne. There she remained until she was thirteen and a half. During her stay at the Convent of the Sacred Heart, no distinction was made between her and the other pupils, the nuns governing the institution being no flatterers of Royalty, accustomed as they had been, for years to educate the daughters of the highest families. To them, the Infanta Eulalia was an ordinary boarder.

While she was still at school, her brother, Alfonso XII., begged his mother, the ex-Queen, to let Eulalia return to Spain, for the young girl was his favourite sister. So to Spain the little princess went, and although, to one of her nature and upbringing, Court life must have been stiff and unpleasant, she remained in Spain until after her brother's death in 1885.

Her homes in Spain were the Escorial and La Granja, and she lived the usual life of a Spanish princess. Of that life nothing need be recorded here. The history of the Infanta Eulalia may be said to begin, for the readers of her book, with her marriage on March 6th, 1886, to Prince Antoine-Louis-Philippe-Marie, Infante of Spain, Duc de Galliera. After her marriage, the Infanta Eulalia again took up her residence in Paris. She has since spent most of her life in France and in England. In the latter country she frequently visited her sister-in-law, the Comtesse de Paris, and many English friends during the London season, being on one occasion the guest of Lord and Lady Clifford of Chudleigh at Ugbrooke.

The year 1893 is a memorable one in the life of the Infanta Eulalia, for it was then that she visited, in company with her husband, Cuba and the United Stales. In Cuba, one of the remnants of the old Spanish Empire—and that, too, soon to be torn away—they were received and entertained with much pomp and ceremony, in accordance with the requirements of Spanish etiquette. In America, most democratic of countries, they mingled freely with the people, and the contact doubtless stirred in the Infanta's mind those liberal ideas concerning men and things which have brought her into such worthy prominence.

While in Cuba the royal visitors were entertained with a bull-fight, six bulls having been imported for the occasion from Spain, and a garden party was given in their honour by Captain-General Rodriguez Arrico at his summer residence, Los Molinos, the party being attended by all the chief officials and the élite of Havana society. The Royal guests also visited the Asylum Beneficencia Domicilirria, were present at a performance at the Albizu Theatre, attended a great military review, and a ball at the Casino Español. On May 15th they sailed for New York on the *Reina Maria Cristina*, having been serenaded the night before by the firemen and volunteers of Havana.

Previous to the departure of the Infante and Infanta from Cuba, the people of Washington, New York, and Chicago, who had been preparing for the visit, were thrown into a state of anxiety by a rumour that the Infanta might not, after all, visit the United States owing to ill-health. Representatives of the newspapers, who called upon the Spanish Minister, Señor Murugua, were told that the Royal lady dreaded the burden of the social functions arranged for her entertainment in the cities she was expected to visit; she had read of the "lionising" of the Duke of Veragua, the lineal descendant of Christopher Columbus, and a noted breeder of bulls for the arena, who had preceded her, and she shrank from the fatigue that would accompany the round of pleasure prepared for one of her rank. The Spanish Court considered that, as the Infanta had been invited by Act of Congress to be the guest of the nation, as representative of the Queen-Regent of Spain, she ought to be received with the honours due to her exalted position. But, when it was learned that the President of the United States refused to return her proposed call, great was Spanish indignation, and it was at one time feared that she would return direct to Spain from Havana. However, the person most concerned disregarded the diplomatic hubbub and left for the States, as already stated.

The *Reina Maria Cristina* arrived in New York late in the night of the 18th of May.

In the morning, the U.S. dispatch-boat *Dolphin*, bearing the representative of the President of the United States, was seen to be lying at anchor just outside Sandy Hook, on the New Jersey coast. It would seem that the *Dolphin* expected the *Reina Maria Cristina* to move into the bay, while the latter awaited the former outside the bar. Etiquette had again crept in. Finally, an understanding was reached through the mediation of the Spanish consul, for it was explained that it was impossible for the Infanta to enter a foreign port in any ship but a Spanish man-of-war, whereupon the *Dolphin* saluted the Infanta with twenty-one guns, and then followed in the wake of the cutter sent for her by the Spanish frigate *Isabel*, on board of which she was received with Royal honours. While on the cruiser, a delegation from the Spanish colony in New York came to welcome her, and to pay her its respects. The ceremony was of the briefest and most formal kind, the visitors being introduced by her chamberlain, the Duc de Tamames. Shortly afterwards, she landed at Jersey City, and entrained thence for Washington.

The Infanta arrived at the capital at eight o'clock the same evening, being met at the station by Secretary Gresham, representing the President of the United States, and by Assistant Secretaries Quincy and Adee, who, after welcoming the nation's guest, conveyed her in the President's state carriage to the Arlington Hotel. Next day, she called on the President at the White

House, and two hours later her call was returned by Mrs. Cleveland and the wives of the members of the Cabinet.

During her brief and enjoyable stay in Washington, the Infanta devoted most of her time to sight-seeing, and visited the home of George Washington at Mount Vernon, on the opposite side of the Potomac. The President and Mrs. Cleveland gave a dinner in honour of Her Royal Highness, and Sir Julian Pauncefote's ball at the British Embassy to celebrate Queen Victoria's birthday was honoured by the Infanta's presence. During her sojourn in the capital, she attended St. Matthew's Church. She naturally was besieged by callers from the Embassies and Legations, as well as by people prominent in social circles of the capital.

On May 25th she left Washington *en route* for New York, and at Jersey City was greeted by committees of the citizens of New York and of the Spanish residents, the principal officers of the Spanish warships in port, and the Spanish consul. On reaching New York she was welcomed by the Mayor (the Hon. Thomas F. Gilroy), and afterwards escorted to the Savoy Hotel. In reply to the address delivered by Mayor Gilroy the Infanta said:

"I am delighted with the graciousness of the pleasant reception you have tendered me. In fact, my welcome has been so hearty and spontaneous that I am confused, and hardly know what to say."

Her round of pleasure was to begin on the very evening of her arrival. While dining, she was greeted with the strains of Spain's "Royal March" from a band stationed on the Piazza, while a group of New York Spaniards cheered vociferously, and clamoured for her appearance. She graciously showed herself on the balcony. When, just as she was returning to the dining-room, she was asked at what hour she desired to go to the theatre, her answer, as recorded by an American journalist, was:

"From nine to ten, to show myself to the people who have been so kind to me; but I should so like to be back at ten o'clock, for I am very tired, and I would like to come home and go to sleep."

On the following day she was entertained at a ball given in her honour in the Concert Hall of Madison Square Garden. It was there that she made an impression that served her well throughout her stay in the United States, her tact and simplicity of manner placing everyone at ease. There had been bitter heart-burnings as to who would be spoken to by the Infanta, and much intriguing had taken place, in order to secure an *entrée* to the charmed Royal circle. These jealousies were dispelled by the Infanta herself, who chatted affably with all, making no invidious distinctions.

"We felt we were *all* hostesses," was the comment of a prominent New York lady.

The Infanta had a busy time in New York. She cruised up the Hudson as far as Yonkers, was taken over Governor's Island in New York Harbour, and the U.S. Military Academy at West Point, attended the review on Decoration Day, and laid a wreath on General Grant's sarcophagus at Riverside. A little incident, which reveals the sympathetic, warm-hearted impulsiveness of the Infanta, occurred when she visited the Normal School, where she was gracefully welcomed by 1,900 girls. In a characteristic outburst of womanly feeling, she exclaimed:

"I can only say that I wish I were sitting on the benches with you, girls."

On June 5th she left for Chicago, and Chicago was determined not to be behind New York and Washington in the enthusiasm of its reception. It had been announced that only the "best society" would be invited to meet the Infanta, and much bad feeling was created when a member of this select coterie, on being asked by a local journalist whether the City Fathers would be invited, unguardedly replied:

"The City Council could hardly claim to represent our best society."

In the end, however, everybody who was or who pretended to be entitled to hobnob with Royalty was invited.

At the Union Depot she was met by Mayor Carter Harrison—so soon to be foully murdered. She speedily became as popular in Chicago as in New York and Washington, and when she visited the Exhibition she was at once named "Queen of the Fair." Her desire for privacy was courteously respected, and on several occasions she was permitted to leave the hotel and to go out for a walk unnoticed. The Duke of Veragua, who was about to leave Chicago, called on her, and a reception was given in her honour at the Mayor's private residence, but on the whole she was left to herself much more than she had been in New York. With visits to the Niagara Falls, Boston, and some of the watering-places on the Atlantic seaboard, this princess of old Spain concluded her stay in the western republic. She left New York on board the *Touraine* for Havre, *en route* for Madrid, carrying with her all the varied impressions which the modern institutions and industrial and social forwardness of the United States had made upon her receptive mind. The following letter to Señor Arturo Cuyas, of the Circulo Colon-Cervantes, New York, written in English the day before her departure, is evidence of the feelings the country aroused in her:—

NEW YORK, 23 JUNE, 1893.

DEAR MR. CUYAS,

Your inquiry about the impressions the United States have produced on my mind have met my expectations (*sic*). They are most favourable and, judging from the present, will be lasting, as so many pleasant remembrances will be attached to them.

It would require more than Longfellow's thorough knowledge of English, Depew's imagination, and Mary Anderson's sentimentality to express all the feelings which I entertain for this country.

The official world, the Press, the people and society at large have been most kind to me.

Let me close with a French saying, "La distance n'est pas l'oubli."

Au revoir!
INFANTA EULALIA

The domestic affairs of the Infanta and her husband about twelve years ago received that undesirable publicity which the "fierce light which beats upon a throne" gives even to those who are only related to its occupant. The result was a rumour that the Royal couple were divorced. This was wholly untrue. The fact was that, by mutual consent and without any intervention on the part of the Courts of Justice, a separation was arranged. By this arrangement, the Infanta continues not only to receive the £6,000 annually voted by the Cortes, but also the allowances under her marriage settlement. Her town residence is in Madrid, and she has a cottage at Navas de Pinares, in the Province of Avila, high up in the Sierra de Malagon, a continuation of the Sierra de Guadarrama. The name Comtesse d'Avila, under which the French edition of this book was published, is taken from the province in which her country residence is situated.

The Infanta has two sons, both of whom were educated, first at Beaumont College, the Jesuit institution near Windsor known as the "Catholic Eton," and later at the Spanish Military Academy at Toledo. The eldest is Prince Alphonse-Marie-François Diego, born in Madrid in 1886. He holds a commission in the infantry regiment of San Fernando. Three years ago he married Princess Beatrice of Saxe-Coburg and Gotha, daughter of the

THE INFANTA EULALIA AT WORK ON
"THE THREAD OF LIFE"

late Duke, better known in this country as the Duke of Edinburgh. The Prince Alfonso served in the recent Melilla campaign, and as late as December of 1911 was received by King Alfonso, who conversed with him about the situation in that Spanish colony on the Moroccan coast. About the same time the King also received the Infanta's second son, Infante Louis-Ferdinand-Marie-Zacarias, who was born at Madrid in 1888.

It will be noticed that the elder brother does not bear the title of Infante of Spain. He was deprived of it on his marriage to a Protestant princess. It has been reported—it cannot be said with what amount of truth—that his mother declared that "her cup of bitterness was full" after the treatment meted out to her son after serving in the Moroccan campaign, for she asserted that a promise had been made that his title should be restored to him if he served efficiently in Morocco.

The chequered career of the Infanta from her earliest childhood—a career almost without precedent in the annals of Royal houses—has given her the wide purviews, the all-embracing, generous sympathy with human joys, woes and strivings, which can be the attributes only of one who, by nature broad-minded, has had the opportunity and the discernment to form her own opinions on the great problems of life. The Royal infant, hurried from a country in revolution; the little Paris schoolgirl in the care of the nuns of the Convent of the Sacred Heart; the young princess receiving her rightful homage at her brother's Court; her visit to the United States, with all that it taught her; the failure of her married life; her unassuming later years in

France, and her frequent visits to her English friends—all these varied experiences contributed to the making of a character some interesting details of which were given by a Paris correspondent to the *Daily Telegraph* on the occasion of the King of Spain's sensational action regarding "The Thread of Life." He wrote as follows:—

"The Infanta Eulalia, of whom I have often heard a good deal through the Cuban and Spanish colonies here, is herself one of the most remarkable examples of the simple life. And many unjust and untrue things have been said of her on that very account. The princess, on the contrary, while being most simple and unaffected in her ways, is a generous, highly intellectual and resolute personality. She read to me the chapter on the cultivation of the will and one's own personal individuality, and interrupted to tell me:

"'I shall conquer. I believe that the most necessary thing in life is to have a personal, properly developed will of one's own. I have always been resolute myself. I have all my life done my own will when I thought it was proper. I reflected well beforehand, and then no one could stop me; and I always conquered, and I shall conquer again.'

"This last was said with a certain amount of defiance. 'Anyway,' she said, 'I am quite prepared for anything they may now do. I know that there has always been an antipathy between me and the Court life. I hate Court life, anyway, because it is so absurd in many of its stiff formalities. It puts a barrier between you and persons of the intellectual world.

"'You may mix with only a certain set of people, who may be the most opposed to you, whom you feel to be unintellectual, and who are incapable of attracting your sympathy. I hate the barrier that would prevent you from free association with men of merit and of understanding just because they are not in Court circles. At Court they have also known for long that I did not care for them. I love my own simple life. Nothing gives me greater pleasure than my little home here in the Boulevard Lannes, facing the beautiful Bois de Boulogne. When I feel like it, I take a ride on my bicycle in the *allées* of the Bois. I frequently take a ride round the lakes all by myself, and come back with a healthy feeling of pleasure after my exercise. I like simple meals and no great fuss about my table. I like to converse with persons of intellect or artistic taste. I love my children and my grandchildren.'"

Probably no one was more surprised than the Infanta herself that her book—which she described to the above-mentioned interviewer as representing "merely my own experience in life"—should so disturb the Court of Madrid. On the 2nd December, 1911, she received in Paris a telegram from her nephew, King Alfonso, couched in the following terms:

"I am astonished to learn from the newspapers that you are publishing a book as the Countess of Avila, and from other information I suppose this will cause a great sensation. I order you to suspend publication till I have seen the book and till you have received my permission to publish it."

The following telegram in reply was sent by the Infanta:

"I am much surprised that the book should be judged before the contents are known. That is a thing which only happens in Spain. Having never liked Court life, from which I have always kept aloof, I take this opportunity to say good-bye to it, for after this proceeding, worthy of the Inquisition, I consider myself free to act in my private life as I think proper."

The text of these telegrams was communicated by the princess to the Paris *Temps*, and, judging from what she said at an interview which she granted to a representative of that journal, there can be no doubt that the bitterness created by the unjust treatment which she declared her soldier son had been subjected to was largely responsible for the definite renunciation of the Court of Madrid to which the telegram gives expression.

The rupture thus created between the King and the Infanta was officially admitted on the 5th of December in the Council of Ministers at Madrid. Throughout early December it formed the paramount topic of conversation in the Spanish capital. The peremptory tone of the Infanta's reply to the King's telegram evoked varied opinions. It was felt by some that her attitude had been unnecessarily defiant, but others regarded it as justifiable resentment of an act of unwarranted interference. The Spanish newspapers were also divided in opinion, but, judging by the number of telegrams and letters of approval and congratulation which arrived at the Infanta's Paris residence, there must have been a very large body of people in her native country who were aroused to enthusiasm by her action.

On the 5th December the Infanta telegraphed as follows to Señor Canalejas, the Spanish Premier:—

"I am awaiting punishment, and I beg you to let me know what it is as soon as possible, since I am about to start on a journey."

To this telegram Señor Canalejas sent the following reply:—

"I have the honour to acknowledge your telegram, and I am to inform you that the Cabinet has so far confined itself to regretting the attitude which you have adopted, as it regards the representations of the head of the Spanish Royal Family as absolutely warranted.—CANALEJAS."

At that time the Government were engaged in discussing the question whether the princess could constitutionally be deprived of her rank of an Infanta of Spain. The payment of her Civil List income was assessed at

250,000 pesetas (about £9,200). The princess, however, estimated her own income at about £6,000, and this estimate was practically confirmed on the 6th December by a semi-official *communiqué*, which asserted that the amount in her Civil List was 150,000 pesetas, i.e. about £5,500. On the solution of the constitutional question of the integrity or otherwise of her rank, the question of the deprivation of her income was known to depend.

The attitude of the King at this time was a fixed determination to act strictly in accordance with the Constitution, though it was understood that in any case the Infanta's personal relations with the Spanish Court would henceforth be regarded as at an end. The princess stated her intention of making a present of her Spanish estates to her eldest son, and of henceforth living *incognito*.

Through the medium of the Paris correspondent of the *Imparcial*, the Infanta addressed a letter to that journal declaring her unaltered affection for Spain, the King, and the Queen-Mother. She said that she would be disposed to ask for pardon, were it not that by so doing she might appear to be anxious about her Civil List. By the 7th December, it appeared improbable that any severe measures would be taken against the Infanta, and the excitement caused in Madrid by the extraordinary incident began to subside.

What was the cause of the attempt by the Spanish Court to stop the publication of "The Thread of Life"? The Infanta herself believed that "the reason they took so much offence was that they imagined it was going to be a book on some other subject—a book that would make a scandal. This was the most remote possible thing from my mind. I had no idea that anyone would trouble about my book. It was for that reason that I had only a small number of copies printed, to be handed round to my friends."

The book was written in French because the Infanta assumed that it would not arouse very much interest in Spain.

"I think," she said to a correspondent of the *Época*, "that the general mode of thought in Spain is not particularly in harmony with the ideas which my book reveals."

The incident, however, has served the useful purpose of drawing the attention of the world to a volume of thoughtful essays by one of the most remarkable personages to be found in the Royal families of Europe—essays which are the more interesting because they are the reasoned conclusions of one who, born and bred in the purple, has emancipated herself from the circumscribed past by contact and sympathy with the wider world of common things.

Milton Keynes UK
Ingram Content Group UK Ltd.
UKHW011229280324
440101UK00007B/692